T0271503

Killer
Collections

Killer Collections

Dark Artifacts *from* True Crime

Paul Gambino

Laurence King Publishing

CONTENTS

INTRODUCTION

Why? But *why*? This book is full of questions—most notably, "why?" Why do people commit such heinous acts of violence? Why were they released only to kill again and again? Why didn't anyone believe she was in danger? Why do certain people seem to be plain evil? Why would someone choose to collect items related to society's darkest and most inhumane moments? To have these items in their *homes*?

Every page of this book is wracked with pain—the pain of losing a loved one; the pain of a loved one being punished for the evil they perpetrated; the pain of punishing oneself for not doing enough, for not being there, or for doing too much. It could be the combination of needing to understand—the "why"—along with empathy with the ensuing pain and sadness that makes true crime so seductive in all its manifestations: TV shows, documentaries, podcasts, books and movies, and the onetime underground but now burgeoning realm of true crime collecting.

The means, motives, and modus operandi for acquiring true crime collectibles can vary significantly within this unique group. Dollar value and the amount a collector is willing to part with can be anywhere from a few dollars to several thousand.

However, very few collect true crime for its monetary value. Although items like John Wayne Gacy paintings have escalated in price and now fetch tens of thousands of dollars, it's the infamous history attached to the piece that will drive the high-profile lawyer to pay whatever the asking price is for a personal item of Charles Manson, and the college student to skip buying lunch for two weeks to snag a signed letter from Richard Ramirez. Some collectors feel the need to possess the physical manifestation of evil—the true crime collectible (or, as it is known in some collector circles, "murderabilia.")

Dig a little deeper into the shallow grave of the human psyche and there are myriad theories as to why we are so obsessed with true crime. Sociologists and philosophers through the ages have suggested that crime is a necessary element in society, with some followers of Freud believing that allowing a small segment of society to partake in violent crime and be punished for it keeps law-abiding citizens in check from acting on their own dark impulses. Others postulate that society's obsession with true crime is ironically a way for them to feel safe; gaining insight into a mind that would perpetrate such heinous acts might allow them to protect themselves and their families from such evil. One interesting theory is that many people drawn to true crime are working through a troubling experience in their own lives, and this is a way for them to help process it. But maybe the fascination is as simple as realizing that we are all just a few bad decisions or fateful encounters away from destroying our own life or the lives of others?

What makes a person who has an interest in true crime take that next step into collecting true crime artifacts, and leap into a world where they not only bring these unsettling items into their homes but also often communicate and develop relationships with the perpetrators of horrible acts of violence that have caused so much pain? I can't speak for the thousands of true crime collectors out there.

However, having put the question, "*Why* do you collect dark artifacts?" to those I interviewed, there was one common theme to their responses. Most consider or rationalize their macabre collections as preserving an important part of our shared history that most of the world would like to pretend didn't exist, confronting humanity's darker side. These items are of historical interest and should be preserved and displayed like other reminders of our past, no matter how ugly that past may be.

There is no denying that true crime collecting is highly controversial. And, although the collectors all agree that their intentions are never to trivialize the pain of the victims and the victims' families, one must accept that at times these pieces are visceral reminders of how their loved ones suffered at the cruel hands of a monster.

Maybe these collections are one way for us to *never* forget that such evil lurks out there— every day and every night.

Paul Gambino

THE ART OF EVIL

It is something of a phenomenon that so many prisoners become "artists" once they find themselves behind bars. There are some apparent reasons: art classes are one of the more encouraged programs offered to prisoners and a way for the incarcerated to pass the endless hours of being locked down. Psychologists say making art allows the prisoner to express their vulnerable feelings through non-verbal communication; it is a means to be honest, offers a necessary diversion and an emotional escape, and re-establishes the person as something other than an inmate. Despite possibly being poorly educated or illiterate, they can still express themselves.

That said, there are people like Samuel Little who paint to perpetuate the evil deeds they inflicted on the outside. Little paints portraits of the women he brutally murdered. On the other hand, Peter Sutcliffe, better known as the Yorkshire Ripper, was a hated man both outside and within the prison system, but his painting reveals a compassionate side at odds with his character. After being attacked and beaten while serving time in multiple prisons for the murder of 13 women, Sutcliffe was moved to Broadmoor psychiatric hospital. There he met a fellow inmate who had been wrongly convicted of murder. Sutcliffe took pity on the man and painted portraits of the man's family members he missed so much. Adam Crutchfield's collection contains one of these very rare original portraits.

Adam is a fine artist, and his sensitivity toward imagery and the visuals evoked from the written word heavily influence his collecting. When asked about his next artwork purchase, he briefly pauses: "I have a soft spot for Gacy paintings. Right now, I'm in search of a Gacy painting entitled 'Skull Clown.' As soon as I can get one, I'm done hunting down Gacy art. They've just become too expensive." Indeed, online auction and collectibles sites are truly making a killing, with Gacy paintings fetching anywhere from $6,000 to $175,000.

Adam has a personal policy he sticks to when acquiring new pieces: "I have no desire in starting a 'friendship' with an inmate to get their art or signed items. I would rather buy the pieces that I'm looking for." This is in stark contrast to many other true crime collectors, who not only enjoy building a personal relationship with an inmate but feel it makes the piece more "intimate."

That lack of desire may come from Adam's fundamental wish to not glorify the murderers or appear to condone the acts of these people. He maintains the utmost respect for the victims and their families and understands the amount of pain left behind within each piece he collects, and that lives have been devastated by these monsters.

The collection of Adam Crutchfield

John Wayne Gacy, Charles Manson, and Ted Bundy are some of the names most people know on their first foray into true crime collecting, and Adam was no exception. His first entry into that world had its pitfalls when he purchased a Gacy signed bookmark at a Nashville tattoo convention for $75. It seemed like a deal too good to be true. Well, he paid the $75 and showed it to a few seasoned collectors. It was, in fact, a deal too good to be true when they told him it was indeed a fake.

The true crime collecting world, like other collecting genres, is plagued with scams and forgeries. However, Adam got off cheaply, and since that initial blunder has curated a significant collection. "I consider myself a collector of items related to crimes with historical significance. If it's not signed artwork, signed letters, etc., from a high-profile case, I don't have much interest. I served in the Army Infantry for almost six years, deployed to both Afghanistan and Iraq. I dealt with loads of combat. I remember that feeling of being surrounded by evil. It was frightening. However, over time I learned to face it and deal with the death and trauma all around me. Then my days became a lot easier. Collecting true crime sort of gives that same feeling of facing evil head-on."

Photos by Dan Howell

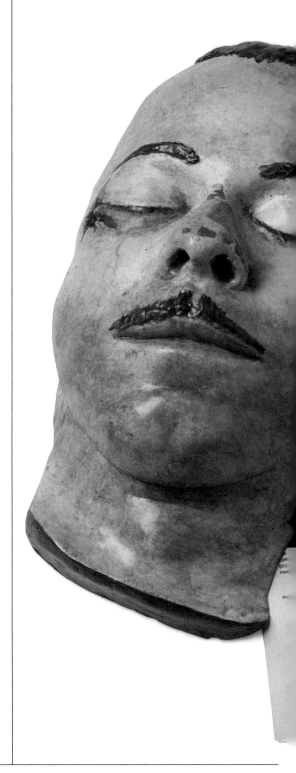

1. Public Enemy #1

As leader of the infamous Depression-era "Dillinger Gang," John Dillinger was accused of robbing 24 banks and four police stations. He was imprisoned several times but escaped twice. Dillinger loved publicity, and the media ran exaggerated accounts of his bravado, painting him as a Robin Hood figure, while the authorities declared him to be public enemy number 1. After being on the run for almost a year, Dillinger returned to Chicago. It was there, on July 22, 1934, that law enforcement closed in and Dillinger was killed when he drew a gun while attempting to flee.

1.1 **Dillinger's print chart and death mask. The FBI struck a death mask of Dillinger at the Cook County morgue. They purportedly took the only mask, but others were made surreptitiously after the FBI officers had left.**

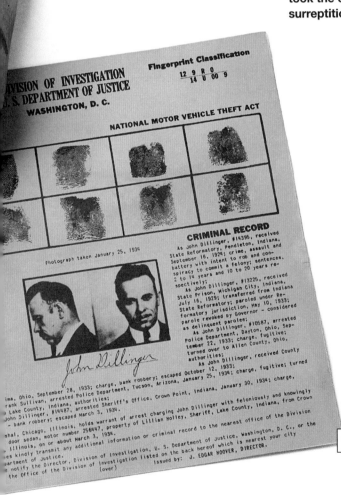

1.1

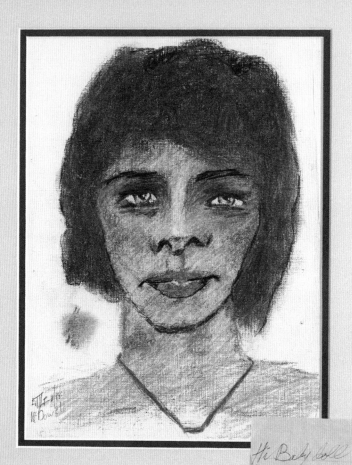

2.1

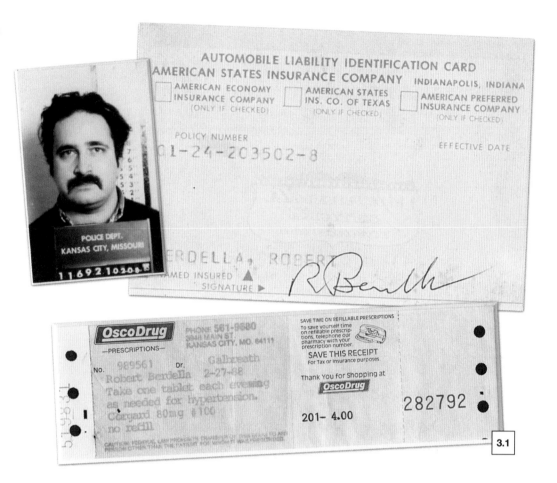

AUTOMOBILE LIABILITY IDENTIFICATION CARD
AMERICAN STATES INSURANCE COMPANY INDIANAPOLIS, INDIANA

☐ AMERICAN ECONOMY INSURANCE COMPANY (ONLY IF CHECKED) ☐ AMERICAN STATES INS. CO. OF TEXAS (ONLY IF CHECKED) ☐ AMERICAN PREFERRED INSURANCE COMPANY (ONLY IF CHECKED)

POLICY NUMBER
01-24-203502-8

EFFECTIVE DATE

ERDELLA, ROBERT
NAMED INSURED ▲
SIGNATURE ▶

POLICE DEPT.
KANSAS CITY, MISSOURI
1 1 6 9 2 1 0 2 0 8

OscoDrug
PHONE 561-9880
3941 MAIN ST.
KANSAS CITY, MO. 64111
—PRESCRIPTIONS—

No. 989561   Dr.   Galbreath
Robert Berdella   2-27-88
Take one tablet each evening
as needed for hypertension.
Corgard 80mg #100
no refill

CAUTION: FEDERAL LAW PROHIBITS TRANSFER OF THIS DRUG TO ANY PERSON OTHER THAN THE PATIENT FOR WHOM IT WAS PRESCRIBED

SAVE TIME ON REFILLABLE PRESCRIPTIONS
To save yourself time
on refillable prescrip-
tions, telephone our
pharmacy with your
prescription number.

SAVE THIS RECEIPT
For Tax or Insurance purposes

Thank You for Shopping at
OscoDrug

201- 4.00

282792

3.1

2. More Than a Little Dangerous

With the FBI linking Samuel Little to 60 murders, he presently holds the title of the most prolific serial killer in US history. However, Little claims to have killed 93.

There were plenty of opportunities to halt the killer before he racked up all these murders. In 1975, when Little was 35, he had already been arrested 26 times in 11 US states. Plus, in 1982 and 1984, he was acquitted on two separate murder charges. Unbeknown to anyone at the time of those acquittals, Little had already killed 23 women.

2.1 An original victim portrait signed by Little, mug shots, plus a letter to his daughter; he writes: "I just got my chocolate bar waiting for you (smile) no peanuts in it. I have been getting your letters, but they were a little late because of a check for poison in all my mail."

3. Murderer's Medication

Robert Berdella, the infamous "Kansas City Butcher," is believed to have killed his first victim on July 5, 1984. He was arrested on April 2, 1988, and eventually found guilty of raping, torturing, and murdering five more victims. Kansas City Police discovered hundreds of Polaroids of his victims as well as log books he had kept of their torture. Berdella died in Missouri State Penitentiary on October 8, 1992, from a heart attack caused by hypertension.

3.1 Berdella's signed automobile insurance card from 1988, police mug shot, and a prescription for hypertension medication, filled 2-27-1988. The prescription is significant as Berdella was arrested just a few weeks later, meaning that this heart medicine was sitting in his home in the midst of the carnage.

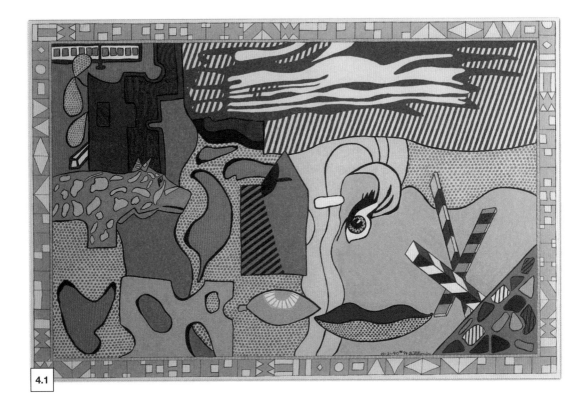

4.1

4. The Freeway Killer

William George Bonin, also known as the Freeway Killer, was an American serial killer and twice-paroled sex offender who between 1979 and 1980 roamed southern California, where he perpetrated the rape, torture, and murder of at least 21 boys and young men. He is also suspected of a further 15 murders. At his first trial, the prosecutor described Bonin as "the most arch-evil person who ever existed."

The level of brutality that Bonin inflicted upon his victims was despicable. One victim was forced to drink hydrochloric acid, three victims had ice picks driven into their ears, and another died of shock while being penetrated anally with a pool cue. Bonin was convicted of 14 of the murders and spent 14 years on death row before he was put to death by lethal injection at San Quentin State Prison in 1996.

4.1 This colorful abstract is just one of an estimated hundred paintings created by the Freeway Killer.

5. The Gainesville Ripper

While serving his time on Florida State Prison's death row for the murder of eight people, Danny Rolling, the "Gainesville Ripper," told fellow inmates his goal was to "become a 'superstar' like Ted Bundy."

Physically and mentally, Rolling was nothing like Bundy. He was neither handsome nor intelligent and was captured (thankfully) after murdering only eight victims, while Bundy had more than 30 murders under his belt before being apprehended. Rolling did, however, focus on raping and killing young, pretty college coeds, a favorite target of Bundy's. They were also both executed, Rolling by lethal injection and Bundy by electrocution.

5.1 An original oil painting made by Danny Rolling c. 1998. An alleged interpretation of the painting is that the tiger represents Rolling, protecting a woman who is rendered to resemble his girlfriend, true crime writer Sondra London.

The Art of Evil

Danny Rolling 98

6.1

6. Death Chant

Before Jim Jones, infamous leader of the Peoples Temple cult, instructed his followers to commit mass suicide in 1978, resulting in 918 Jonestown members' deaths, Jones had felt that music was an important part of the spiritual experience. A former choir member said: "They were singing because they had hope. They had a hope for a better world."

6.1 **An unopened record made by the People's Temple Choir. Two original press photos, an original propaganda piece, an envelope from Jim Jones's desk, and his personal business card.**

7. Waco Schoolwork

David Koresh, the psychotic cult leader of the Waco chapter of the Branch Davidians sect, had poor study skills and dyslexia. His learning disabilities forced him into special education classes, and Koresh eventually dropped out of high school. As head of his cult, he demanded his followers do their schoolwork.

7.1 **Pages of Koresh-approved schoolwork. These are very rare and were purchased directly from a Branch Davidian survivor.**

8. Bracelet from the Boston Strangler

Albert DeSalvo, "the Boston Strangler," was a ladies' man. Unfortunately, he killed 13 women to show his "love." On November 25, 1973, DeSalvo was found stabbed to death in the infirmary at Walpole maximum-security prison, where he was serving times for other crimes.

While no one was ever officially tried for the crimes of the Boston Strangler, DeSalvo confessed to them while already serving a life sentence for a series of rapes; in 2013, almost half a century after the murderous attacks, DNA evidence confirmed DeSalvo's involvement in at least one of them, the killing of Mary Sullivan.

8.1 **Given the nature of his crimes, it follows that DeSalvo would pass his time creating items that appealed to women. This original piece of jewelry, made in a prison shop class by DeSalvo, is labeled "Genuine 'Blue Goldstone' Bracelet."**

'They were singing because they had hope. They had a hope for a better world.'

MEMORY VERSE: "For the time is come that judgment must begin at the house of God: and if it first begin at us, what shall the end be of them that obey not the gospel of God?" 1 Peter 4:17.

STUDY HELP: Branch Lesson No. 7, May 25, 1958. (attached to last month's lessons)

STUDY AIM: To show that the message of Revelation 18:1 comes first to the church before going to the world in the Loud Cry.

INTRODUCTION: "Prophecy must be fulfilled. The Lord says: 'Behold, I will send you Elijah the prophet before the coming of the great and dreadful day of the Lord.' Somebody is to come in the spirit and power of Elijah,..." T.M. 475.

1.   What is the purpose behind the coming of the promised Elijah? Matt. 17:11; Mal. 4:4,5.

Note --- "'Elias truly shall first come and restore all things.' Matt. 17:11. Inevitably, then, without his message we would die in our ignorance and in our sins -- never live to see the restoration completed." G.C.S. 22.

2.   What is Elijah's message to do? G.C.S. 12,13.

Note --- "The day of the Lord, we are told in these verses (Mal. 3:1-3), is a d[...] fining, of purifying, of sifting...All may for a surety know both 'the day' and t[...] as he proclaims it, because to our surprise he will point out that all the prophe[...] the day and also tell what the Lord would have us do (keep the feasts - 1 Cor. [...] while it is approaching and subsequently while we are going through it, and be[...] one but Elijah can proclaim the day." G.C.S. 12,13. (paren. added)

3.   What is the message of Elijah? B.L. #7, p. 5.

Note --- "...since the last work on earth is the Judgment of the Living, the tr[...] forth like the light of day that Elijah's message is the message of the Judgmen[...] Living, the last,..." G.C.S. 25,26.

4.   Where is his message to be presented? G.C.S. 25.

Note --- "...the promised Elijah is to be the last prophet to the church today[...]

5.   How will it be received? G.C.S. 7,8.

Note --- "It is therefore only to be expected that the predicted Elijah will be[...] as a false prophet, perhaps even as the anti-Christ, or what not." G.C.S. 7[...]

     "Everything that can be done will be done to distort the Truth and th[...] and dishearten believers and draw their attention to something other than the [...] of Elijah." G.C.S. 8.

     "Somebody is to come in the spirit and power of Elijah, and when he appears, men may say: 'You are too earnest, you do not interpret the Scriptures in the proper way. Let me tell you how to teach your message.'" T.M. 475,476.

6.   How does this correspond to the reception given the angel of Rev. 18:1?

Ans.--- "In 1888 in the General Conference held at Minneapolis, Minn., the angel of Revelation 18 came down to do his work, and was ridiculed, criticized, and rejected, and when the message he brings again will swell into a loud cry, it will be ridiculed, and spoken against, and rejected by the majority." E. G. White - "In Taking up a Reproach".

7.1

SPECIAL REPORT

TIME

TRAGEDY IN WACO

"His name was Death, and Hell followed with him."
Revelation 6:8

Genuine "Blue Goldstone" Bracelet

Handmade by Albert DeSalvo

8.1

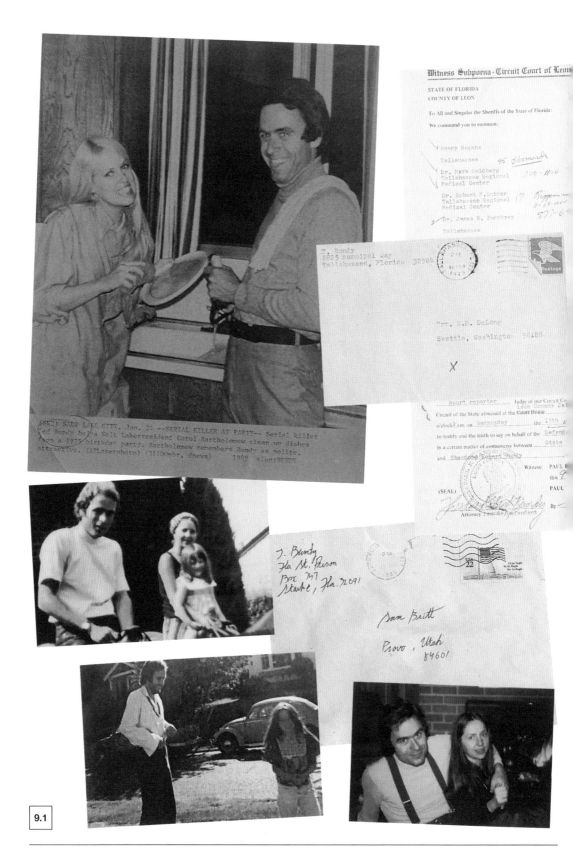

The Art of Evil

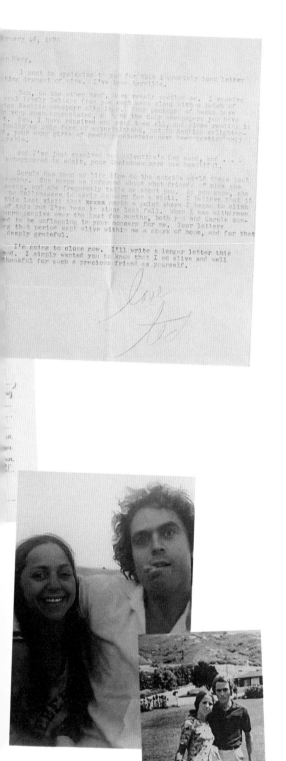

9. A Clear Sociopath

Despite being a convicted rapist and serial killer, Ted Bundy was deluged with pen-pal requests while incarcerated. Professionals who have analyzed his correspondence state: "the letters reveal that Bundy is intelligent, educated and a 'clear sociopath,' who 'completely disassociates himself from the heinous actions he's done in the past' ...
He speaks about his family as if he were a normal and loving person, even though he's left a trail of 30 brutally murdered women in his wake."

9.1 An original press photo and signed court document from Bundy's 1978 trial, snapshots, and a hand-signed letter sent to a pen pal from February 1979, in which Bundy writes: "Carole has been my lifeline to the outside world these last few months. She keeps me informed about what friends of mine she has seen, and she frequently tells me about you." Would you really want to be the subject of a Ted Bundy conversation?

10. Manson's Dark Art

Even before infamous cult leader Charles Manson formed the "Family" and orchestrated the murders of nine people, he fancied himself a creative genius and dabbled in many art media, including painting, sculpture, and string art.

10.1 Signed Manson art pieces, postcard, xerox copy of the Manson Girls, titled "Charlie's Real Angels," and original string art of a spider and a scorpion. [Over the page.]

'The letters reveal that Bundy is intelligent, educated, and a "clear sociopath"'

Charlie's Real Angels

Charles Manson

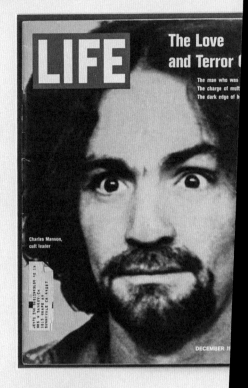

LIFE

The Love
and Terror C

The man who was
The charge of mult
The dark edge of h

Charles Manson,
cult leader

DECEMBER 19

Yes I read your letter, but I can't
keep up on all the dust in the wind
Love your wife + family—Man don't look
up to me thats not me you put fear in
me—I'm NOT what people said
since you can see that I TRUST
NO MAN— I TRUST my BIG
Toe because he's been there
under + understands how much TRUTH is
EASY

MANSON FAMILY
Deceased Cult Leader
CHARLES MANSON
Authentic
Hair Sample

Limited Edition Relic
From
TRUE CRIME AUCTION HOUSE

11. Poisonous Pen Pal

Richard Speck was convicted at trial and originally sentenced to death for murdering eight student nurses in 1966 in such a frenzy that he failed to notice one of the apartment's inhabitants had managed to hide, and would later identify him. His sentence was later changed to 1,200 years behind bars, and he died of a heart attack in 1991. In 1996 a video surfaced from Illinois's Stateville Correctional Center, recorded in the 1980s and "starring" an effeminate-looking Speck, who was allegedly taking hormone treatments. The video featured Speck snorting cocaine, parading in silk panties, sporting female-like breasts, and performing oral sex on another male inmate.

11.1 **In this letter from Speck to one of his pen pals, he laments about his finances: "I make 30 a month in here painting the prison, and I use that for cigarettes, soup, and shampoo, stuff like that, and 30 dollars don't go very far."**

12. Guilty as Charged

After Aileen Wuornos was arrested, convicted, and sentenced to death for the killing of seven men in Florida between 1989 and 1990, she never disputed killing her victims, claiming it was always in self-defense.

12.1 **An envelope containing a letter Aileen wrote from death row to her childhood friend Dawn Botkins, asking her to give it to the prosecutor to admit her guilt and bring a close to the cases: "They sentenced me properly—as I'd only kill again ... I lied—trying to beat the system, so what's the point! There is none, except that it's time to close up shop and execute." The swatch of red fabric is a piece from her last rites robe.**

'They sentenced me properly—as I'd only kill again ...'

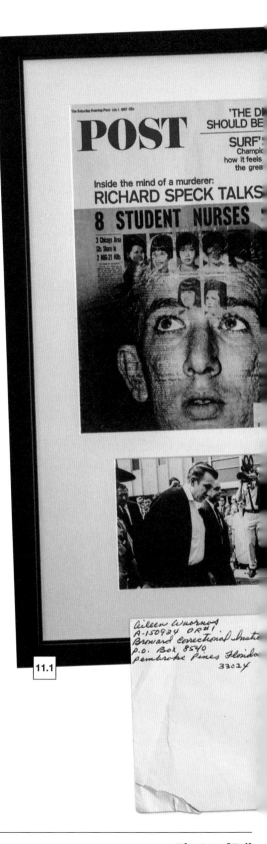

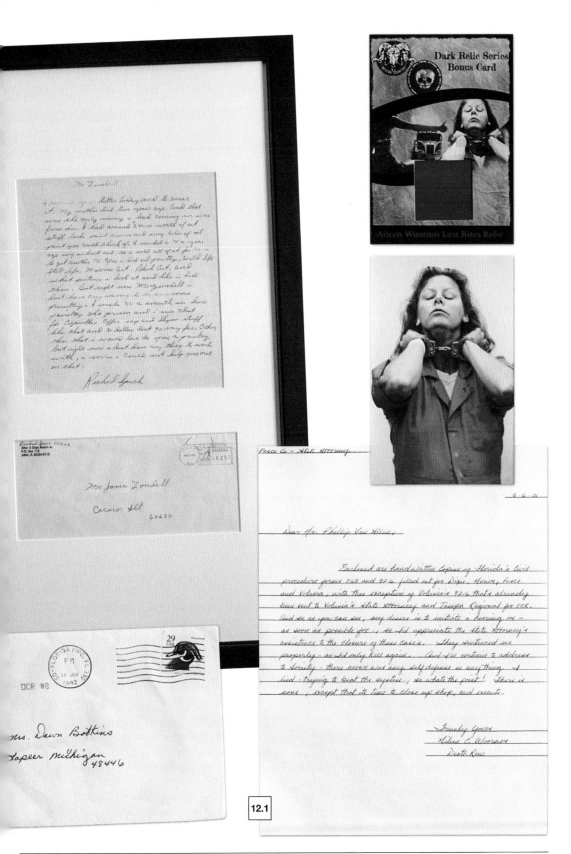

Mr Zundell

I received your letter today and to answer
it. My mother died two years ago. And that
was the only money I had coming in was
from her. I had around $2000 worth of art
stuff lack paint canvas and every color of oil
paint you could think of. I needed 6 to a year
ago my art sent out, so I sold all that for home
to get surtile 70. Yes. I did oil painting, wild life
still life, movie art, black art, and
what suction i look at and like i did
then. But right now Mr Zundell i
dont have anymore to do anymore
painting. I make 30 a month in here
painting the prison and i use that
for cigarettes coffee soap and thing stuff
like that and 30 dollar dont go very far. Other
than that i would love to do you a painting
but right now i dont have anything to work
with, i sorie. could not help you out
on that.

Richard Speck

Mr James Zundell

Cicero All

60650

Pasco Co - State Attorney.

6.6.91

Dear Mr. Phillip Van Allen,

Enclosed are handwritten copies of Florida's civil
procedure forms 760 and 92.6 filled out for Dixi, Marion, Pasco
and Volusia, with the exception of Volusia's 92.6 that's already
been sent to Volusia's State Attorney and Tampa Regional for CCR.
And so as you can see, my desire is to initiate a hearing on –
as soon as possible for , so I'd appreciate the State Attorney's
assistance to the closure of these cases. They sentenced me
properly - as I'd only kill again . And I'll continue to address
to society - there never was any self defense in anything. I
lied - trying to beat the system , so whats the point ! There is
more , except that its time to close up shop, and execute.

Truely Yours
Aileen C Wuornos
Death Row

DCR #8

Mrs. Dawn Botkins

Lapeer Michigan
48446

12.1

Hello Brother Richard,
    Received your letter and i was glad to hear from you. Sure hope this will reach you doing o.k. As for as my self i'm o.k. Well it looks like you have a few things going for you and i think you should keep on them to move you out like you said. Well we are having some problems over here. The night supervisor that comes on at 10:30 is having a hard time. Brother Richard you no if he was wrong i'd say so in a minute. The old man will do anything he can to help anyone, but some of these blacks don't like him and they is trying to get him run off. What i think it is they have 3 or 4 assistant black supervisors on the first shift and i think maybe one of them has put it in these guys head to have the whiteman run off and he would get moved up to take the job. Brother Richard if it had'nt been for this old man last year i would have died here in the hole. I no i owe him my life, and i can't stand to see him shit on. You take care and you be careful as that guy may pay some one to mess you up. You no how these blacks works. Brother Richard don't worry i no what i'm doing. By the way the other day Pop McCormick got a visit and he told them what happoned to me and seen John T. O'Neal about said if he did'nt do nothing

Donald H. Gaskins
1515. Gist St. M.S.C.
Columbia. S.C. 2920-

By Donald H. "Pee Wee" Gaskins

13.1

13. The Redneck Charles Manson

In addition to "Pee Wee," Donald Henry Gaskins Jr. had a list of other more notorious monikers, including "the Meanest Man in America" and "the Redneck Charles Manson." Gaskins had a rough childhood, with family neglect that resulted in him drinking a bottle of kerosene when he was just one year old. As a young boy Gaskins was put into reform schools for a multitude of crimes, including gang rape.

While serving a life sentence for eight murders in South Carolina Correctional Institution, Gaskins was hired to kill Rudolph Tyner, a fellow inmate who had killed an elderly couple. He killed Tyner via an elaborate scheme that included C-4 plastic explosives and a portable radio. When Tyner put the radio to his ear, Gaskins detonated the explosives from his cell. Gaskins said, "The last thing he [Tyner] heard was me laughing." Gaskins was convicted and sentenced to death for the murder of Tyner – the first time in the history of South Carolina that a white man was sentenced to death for murdering a black man. Gaskins was executed via the electric chair on September 6, 1991.

13.1 A letter Gaskins sent to a pen pal: "Brother Richard, if it hadn't been for this old man last year, I would have died here in the hole. I know I owe him my life, and I can't stand to see him shit on." Also, a signed photo of Gaskins with a friend, original Gaskins artwork, and prison money from his jail in South Carolina.

Would Then go TO The NEWS PAPER ABout it.
IN Case You ever WANT To CALL The NEWS PAPER, ASK
FoR HOLLY GATLING - 771-8413. She is A good FRiend OF
MiNE. They WANT let me CALL heR over here.
BRother RichARd do You No STeve CHAPMAN THere iN
C-B-2. You No he ANd DoNNie GRiffiN WAS Accused OF
KiLLiNG Doc Hughes iN C-B-3. The ReAsoN i WANT To No
is i heARd ThAT STeve got 9-YeARS FoR it. STeve is
A good FRiend OF mine, WhAT i WANT You to FiNd
out FRom him WhAT did DoNNie GRiffiN got. He
is over here ANd uP StAiRS ANd WANT Tell No
one whAt he got, AS You No i don't have NothiNG
To do with him No WAY As he WAS The CAuse i
Could Not ever get out OF C-B-2. Well MY
good FRiend i'm goiNG to Cut this oNe short
BY SAYiNG TAke CARe ANd Keep PRAYiNG ANd
i wish You The VeRY Best oN everYthiNG, So
uNTil Next Time Be Cool.

        Your Brother in Christ.
        Donald H. Dewie Garling

PETER SUTCLIFFE

14.1

PWS
C90

14. Pitied by the Yorkshire Ripper

On May 22, 1981, Peter Sutcliffe was found guilty of murdering 13 women and attempting to murder seven others. Sutcliffe, who had been dubbed the Yorkshire Ripper by the press, was sentenced to 20 concurrent life sentences.

While incarcerated at HM Prison Parkhurst, Sutcliffe was attacked multiple times by fellow inmates and, despite being found sane at his trial, in March 1984 he was sent to Broadmoor, a high-security psychiatric hospital. Here Sutcliffe continued to be attacked, and after one incident he lost the use of his left eye, and his right eye was severely damaged.

In Broadmoor Sutcliffe met Larry Perry, a fellow inmate convicted of attempting to kill his wife and, despite the gun being fake, he was given a life sentence. Perry's family disowned him and refused to see or speak to him. When Perry lamented to Sutcliffe how much he loved and missed his children, Sutcliffe took pity and painted portraits of Perry's children to comfort him. Seventeen years into his sentence, a social worker looked into Perry's case and was convinced he should never have been convicted and sentenced. She spearheaded an investigation, and Perry was eventually released.

14.1 One of the paintings that Sutcliffe made of Larry Perry's son, presumably from a school photograph. The other photo shows a true crime trading card from 1992.

Charles Milles Manson

November 12, 1934 - November 19, 2017

"I never thought I was normal.
I never tried to be normal."

than this,
on his life
nds.

- John 15:13

I can do all things through
Christ which strengtheneth me.

- Philipians 4:13

In Loving M
Charles Mille

Enter
Nover
Cir

En
N
B

12:00
Porterville

A CURATOR OF CRIME

The 30-year period from the 1970s through the 1990s has been deemed the golden age of serial killers by some criminologists, with 88 percent of all known twentieth-century American serial killers making an appearance then, including Ted Bundy, Jeffrey Dahmer, Gary Ridgway, John Wayne Gacy, David Berkowitz, and Richard Ramirez.

Data compiled by Mike Aamodt of Radford University cites nearly 770 serial killers who operated in the United States throughout the 1980s, and just under 670 in the 1990s. In the 2000s, the number fell below 400, and as of 2015, it was estimated that there were just over a hundred. The decline is linked to many factors, including helicopter parenting and advances in forensics/DNA detection, which allow law enforcement to quickly connect a killer to a crime scene.

Based on the thousands of true crime artifacts in Anthony Meoli's remarkable collection, you would not imagine any shortage of high-profile crime in the near future. However, the huge volume of material can be attributed to Anthony's connection with the people in lockup. He began to contact inmates shortly after graduating from Penn State University with a degree in criminology, in an effort to better understand why these people did what they did. This contact eventually led to Anthony developing a rapport and, ultimately, relationships with scores of inmates.

For the better part of 20 years, Anthony would spend hours every week receiving inmate calls from penal institutions located throughout the United States, from such high-profile murderers as Manson, Ramirez, Malvo, Henley, and Bianchi. Anthony also left the safety of his suburban Pennsylvania home to visit serial killers on death row, including Glen Rogers, Danny Rolling, and Loran Cole, to name just a few. Some of the relationships he developed became so close that many inmates have painted portraits of him. One, James Edward Ruzicka, who has been deemed a sexual psychopath and is serving two life sentences for rape and murder, has entrusted Anthony to carry out the wishes of his last will and testament.

Anthony sees a bleak future when it comes to traditional mail correspondence with prisoners behind bars: "Inmate writing, meaning handwritten letters, will be disappearing entirely over the next five to ten years. Email is the new way most inmates prefer to communicate, and that all adds up to the handwritten word disappearing. All the more reason to collect history now, as it is slowly disappearing right before our eyes."

The collection of Anthony Meoli

ANTHONY MEOLI, MA, J.D., NCC.

Over the last two decades, Anthony has collected thousands of items, with most coming directly from the inmate or someone close to them. Some are tokens of relationships he has developed, while other pieces are by-products of books or projects.

Anthony views the items as corporeal artifacts. "I do not consider anything I own a 'prized' possession. These men and women ruined many lives. As for the rarest items, I would say the sneakers Aileen Wuornos was wearing when arrested and one of Charles Manson's acoustic guitars."

Anthony's diverse professional life as a forensic consultant, author, and board-certified counselor has given him a unique perspective on true crime collecting. He can see how people might be offended by certain items, but adds that he "can probably remember and name more of the victims of violent crime than most people on the planet—simply because these items constantly remind me of them. They do not haunt me; they serve as reminders of the crimes that those who say it is immoral have long forgotten."

Anthony won't deal with gang members or people who have committed hate crimes. For him, that group of offenders is off-limits for contact or collecting.

Photos by Dan Howell

1.1

1. Whitey the Mob Rat

Whitey Bulger was an Irish American mob crime boss and FBI informant who, despite killing 19 people, became something of a folk hero as he evaded capture for 16 years. One of the last of the old-school Boston gangsters, Bulger was eventually apprehended in June 2011 and handed two life sentences.

On October 30, 2018, guards found 89-year-old Bulger dead. He was slumped in his wheelchair, having been beaten to death by multiple inmates wielding a padlock wrapped in a sock and a prison shank. His eyes had almost been gouged out and his tongue nearly cut off. Some people never escape ratting on the mob.

1.1 Sneakers worn by the infamous mobster, who would only wear clothes for short periods before throwing them away. The glass oil and vinegar set was on Whitey's kitchen table when he was arrested. Both items were obtained through the U.S. Marshals Service.

This is to certify that the enclosed item(s) is genuine and 100% authentic

I, _____ was a victim of the Aurora Theater Massacre on July 20, 2012- shortly after midnight on the night of July 19, 2012.

I was attending the midnight premiere of *Batman: The Dark Knight Rises* at the Century 16 Theater in Aurora, CO when a gunman entered the theater and threw tear gas canisters into the crowd (one of which landed at my feet). As soon as I recognized the odor of the gas, I began my exit from the theater, at which point the shooter - suspected to be James Holmes - fired shotgun blasts full of birdshot at myself and other patrons inside the theater.

Despite having over 22 wounds from the birdshot, I made it out of the theater and was taken to a nearby hospital for care. Many of the pellets in my body did not cause complications until much later, and in late September of 2014, I had two of them removed from my body. One was sinking into the ribs in my chest, and the other was causing a lump in my right arm.

This event has been covered by various media outlets, many of whom have covered my name and story very extensively. A quick Google search would quickly verify that I was indeed a survivor of the shooting and that these pellets are 100% authentic.

I am one of at least 40 counts of attempted murder in the case; I hereby swear that these items are 100% authentic pellets from the shotgun allegedly used by James Holmes in the shooting, and later surgically removed from my body.

Signed,

14 JANUARY 2015

2.1

3.1

2. Flowers for the Departed Souls?

Seventeen-year-old Elmer Wayne Henley was a reluctant yet cooperating participant in the rape, torture, and murder of over 28 teenage boys and young men at the hands of 33-year-old Dean Corll. However, on the night of August 8, 1973, Henley's conscience got the best of him, and as Corll was about to rape his next victim, Henley shot Corll to death. Despite being so young and having been manipulated by Corll, Henley was sentenced to 594 years in prison.

2.1 Original artwork by Elmer Wayne Henley. Henley is one of the few serial killer artists who does not paint violent imagery, even if requested. The State of Texas took away his painting privileges several years ago, so he can no longer paint.

3. Pellet from the Victim of a Mass Shooting

July 20, 2012, was the date of a mass shooting inside a Century 16 movie theater in Aurora, Colorado, during a midnight screening of the film *The Dark Knight Rises*. Decked out in tactical gear, James Eagan Holmes detonated tear-gas grenades and then fired into the audience with multiple firearms. Twelve people were killed, and 58 others were injured directly from his gunfire.

3.1 This shotgun pellet was obtained directly from a victim who survived the shooting and sold off pellets removed from her body. The collector was willing to donate the fee. Still, she insisted on sending him the pellet to express her appreciation, and to show how the loss of the pellet empowered her to go on and not define herself as a victim.

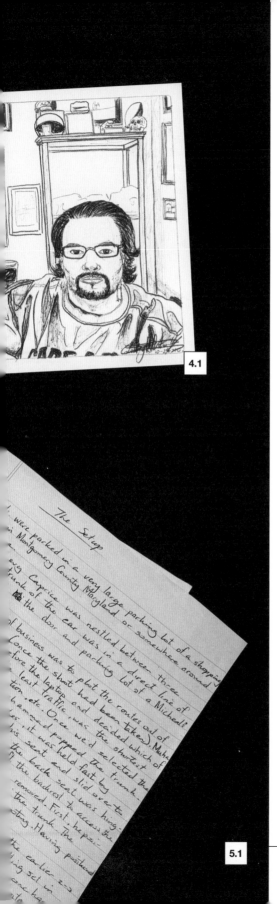

4.1

5.1

4. Killer Commissions

The close personal relationships Anthony has developed with inmates are reflected in the fact that several have made portraits of him. The piece by Lee Boyd Malvo was for a book Anthony was writing, while the other two were given as gifts, based on personal visits or pictures he had sent. Says Anthony: "It is odd to see how you look to someone else—particularly when the three combined have a known death toll of over 35 people."

4.1 The red and black painting was made by "the Cross Country Killer," Glen Rogers; Elmer Wayne Henley, accomplice to the "Candy Man" Dean Corll, created the charcoal portrait; the ink portrait was done by Lee Boyd Malvo, the "D.C. Sniper."

5. Diary of the D.C. Sniper

Lee Boyd Malvo was only 17 when he was arrested along with 42-year-old John Allen Muhammad on October 24, 2002, for the spree killing of ten people between February and October that year, dubbed the Beltway Sniper attacks. Muhammad was executed for the murders in 2009, while Malvo is serving life without the possibility of parole.

5.1 A handwritten 225-page "diary" of Lee Boyd Malvo, sent directly from Malvo to the collector. "Over a six-year period, I wrote and spoke on the phone to Malvo over 200 times before he released his diary to me. Malvo also drew all the original artwork, including the cover, for my book."

'It's odd to see how you look to someone else— particularly when the three combined have a known death toll of over 35 people.'

6.1

6. The Killer Clown

John Wayne Gacy, "the Killer Clown," first gained infamy for murdering over 30 young men and burying them under his house. Before he was executed via lethal injection on May 10, 1994, he became a highly prolific behind-bars fine artist whose work was in high demand, particularly those featuring his alter ego, Pogo the clown.

6.1 This Gacy piece, entitled "Stuart Wall," was commissioned by its original owner in 1984, but he was too creeped out by it and sold it shortly after. It is widely considered among the Stradivarius (rarest and most covetable) of Gacy paintings due to the celebrities and true crime collectors who have owned it. It depicts Gacy's alter ego standing in a cemetery, which was unusual as Gacy always denied his guilt.

'Considered among the Stradivarius (rarest and most covetable) of Gacy paintings due to the celebrities and true crime collectors who have owned it.'

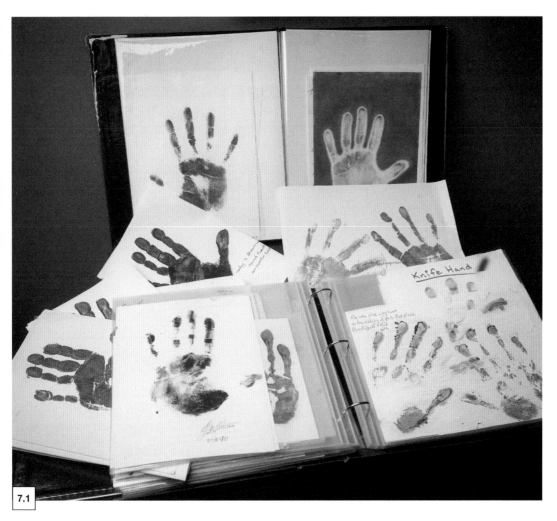

7.1

7. The Hand of Death

Many policing agencies do not take palm prints of inmates when arrested, Anthony notes. "Given the number of cold cases that partial prints have solved, I have always found these to be possible tools. I also compare the proportion of a given inmate's hands to their height and weight. The fingerprints also yield injuries, cuts, and attributes such as the types of fingerprints: Arch (2 types), Whorl (3 common types), Loops (3 common types). Arch fingerprints are only present in about 5 percent of all fingerprints, making them very rare among offenders."

7.1 Over 190 handprints of serial killers and murderers, obtained by the collector as examples of physical artifacts and used for forensic purposes.

8. Born Again

The owners of the Bibles pictured on the following pages were responsible for the brutal murder of over 19 people between them. But like so many ruthless killers, after being incarcerated—especially having spent years in 23-hour lockdown—they found religion.

8.1 The personal Bibles of Christine Falling, Lawrence Bittaker, Aileen Wuornos, Whitey Bulger, and Mark David Chapman. Those belonging to Chapman and Bittaker were obtained directly from the inmates; the others were collected from various individuals related to or acquainted with the inmates. [Over the page.]

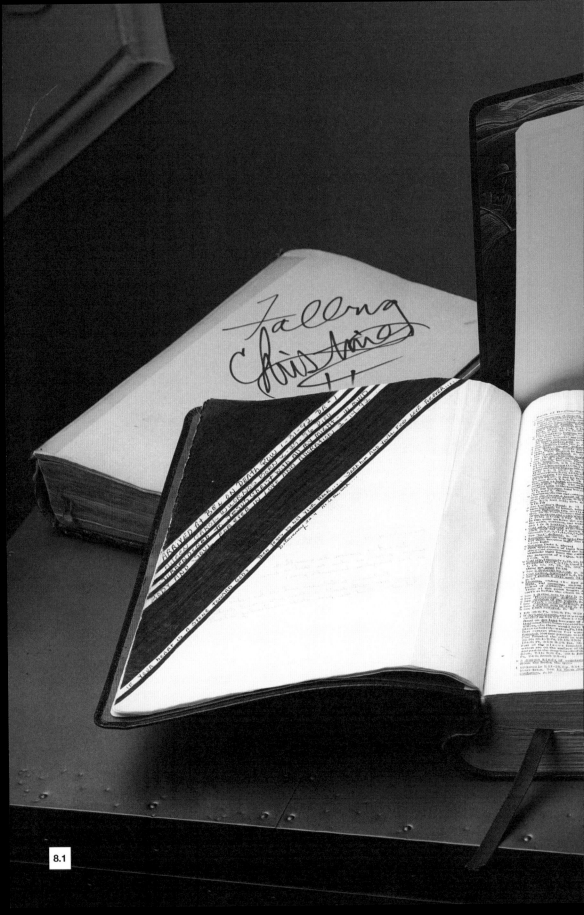

8.1

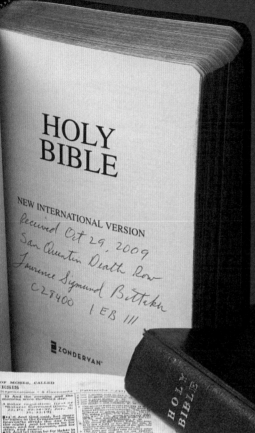

9.1

9. The Hillside Strangler

It has been over 40 years since Kenneth Bianchi and his cousin Angelo Buono Jr. were tried and convicted of the torture, rape, and murder of 12 young women in what the California media labeled the Hillside Strangler murders. However, Bianchi still maintains his innocence and files countless appeals. He was recently quoted as saying: "The most frustrating part about all of this for me is the real killer(s) was never charged, and I've spent 40 years in jail for crimes I did not commit. I can't point to just one thing as the gravest error in my case; there are so many egregious errors."

9.1 Watercolor created by Bianchi for Anthony. "He wanted to incorporate imagery of childhood memories that I had shared. The tree symbolized large trees I had climbed as a kid. The concrete was a creek where I played. The picket fence was how he saw my childhood (with two parents and a brother), and the winged horse monster is a representation of the 'Jersey Devil' (since I grew up in New Jersey)."

9.2 An original watercolor, entitled "Christ," created by Bianchi as the collector helped Kenneth work through the passing of his mother while he questioned his faith. The piece incorporates over 150,000 circles to make the image appear whole, and it was obtained directly from Bianchi.

'He wanted to incorporate imagery of childhood memories that I had shared.'

9.2

Kenneth Alessio Bianchi
5 August 11

10.1

10. The Fine Art of Murder

Gary Mark Gilmore was sentenced to death for two senseless killings. On July 19, 1976, he robbed and murdered Max Jensen, a gas station attendant, in Orem, Utah, and the following night robbed and murdered Bennie Bushnell, a motel manager, in Provo, despite both men complying with Gilmore's demands. During his trial, he asked that the death penalty, only recently reintroduced in the U.S., be implemented. On January 17, 1977, Gilmore was transported to an abandoned cannery behind Utah State Prison, which served as its death house, and executed by firing squad.

10.1 Rare paintings and ink sketches by Gilmore, who had studied art at a community college before being convicted.

11. Gifts from a Psychopath

In 1974, while undertaking a compulsory rehabilitation program after attacking two Seattle women, Jim Ruzicka managed to escape from the Western State Hospital. Ruzicka had been diagnosed as a sexual psychopath, and while on the run he raped and strangled two teenage girls to death. Later, while in prison for the separate crime of raping a 13-year-old girl, Ruzicka admitted to the murder of the two girls and was ultimately sentenced to two consecutive life terms.

11.1 Ruzicka created this piece from over 15,000 beads strung together on fishing line and then stitched to the leather backing. The design, depicting Pogo the clown—the persona created by serial killer John Wayne Gacy—is very complex and took over five months to create. The collector provided Ruzicka with the materials.

11.2 The last will and testament of Jim Ruzicka. "Ruzicka and I have gotten very close over more than a half dozen years, and he shared many things never before known to police. To that end, he was afraid of what the state would do with his body. Jim wishes to have certain things done upon his death to prepare him for the next life. He asked whether I would take possession of his body upon his death. While it was an extremely unusual request, it was hard to turn down knowing I was the only person who knew and could fulfill his last wishes. This is the will that was signed, duly witnessed, and notarized by the State of Washington."

11.3 Ruzicka played this guitar in his cell for three years before sending it to the collector. It is adorned with Ruzicka's trademark skulls, and his signature appears on the back. Ruzicka applied countless layers of floor wax obtained from the prison to protect the artwork, resulting in a lacquer-like finish.

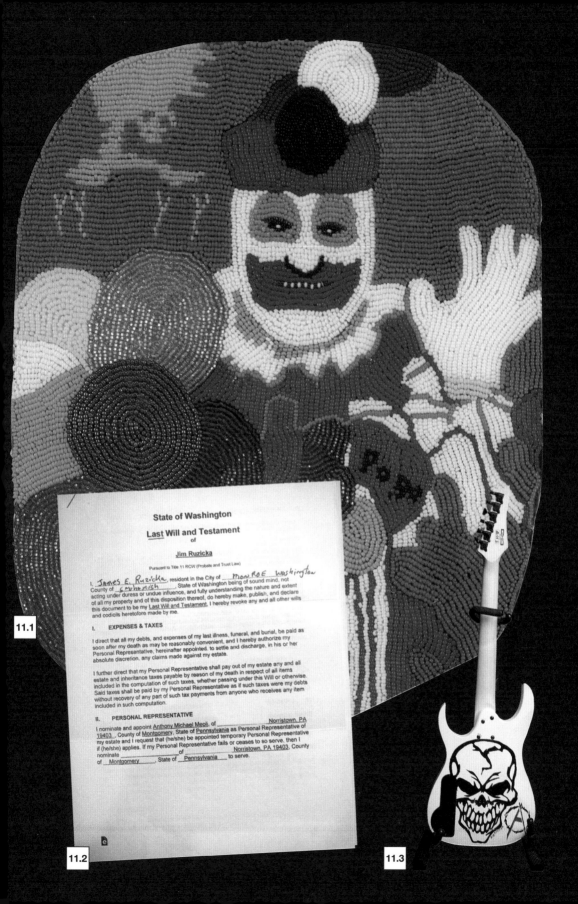

11.1

11.2

State of Washington

Last Will and Testament

of

<u>Jim Ruzicka</u>

Pursuant to Title 11 RCW (Probate and Trust Law)

I, <u>James E. Ruzicka</u>, resident in the City of <u>Monroe Washington</u>
County of <u>Snohomish</u>, State of Washington being of sound mind, not
acting under duress or undue influence, and fully understanding the nature and extent
of all my property and of this disposition thereof, do hereby make, publish, and declare
this document to be my <u>Last Will and Testament</u>, I hereby revoke any and all other wills
and codicils heretofore made by me.

I.   EXPENSES & TAXES

I direct that all my debts, and expenses of my last illness, funeral, and burial, be paid as
soon after my death as may be reasonably convenient, and I hereby authorize my
Personal Representative, hereinafter appointed. to settle and discharge, in his or her
absolute discretion. any claims made against my estate.

I further direct that my Personal Representative shall pay out of my estate any and all
estate and inheritance taxes payable by reason of my death in respect of all items
included in the computation of such taxes, whether passing under this Will or otherwise.
Said taxes shall be paid by my Personal Representative as if such taxes were my debts
without recovery of any part of such tax payments from anyone who receives any item
included in such computation.

II.   PERSONAL REPRESENTATIVE

I nominate and appoint <u>Anthony Michael Meoli</u>, of _____ <u>Norristown, PA</u>
<u>19403</u> , County of <u>Montgomery</u>, State of <u>Pennsylvania</u> as Personal Representative of
my estate and I request that (he/she) be appointed temporary Personal Representative
if (he/she) applies. If my Personal Representative fails or ceases to so serve, then I
nominate _____ of _____ <u>Norristown, PA 19403</u>, County
of ___<u>Montgomery</u>___, State of ___<u>Pennsylvania</u>___ to serve.

11.3

12. Head of the Family

One of the most recognized faces in true crime history, and highly prized among collectors, Charles Manson was born on November 12, 1934, to 16-year-old Kathleen Manson. At the age of 14, he committed his first known crime by robbing a grocery store. After a series of juvenile lockups and psychiatric stays, where he was brutalized, Manson got married in 1955.

For the next decade, Manson was in and out of lockups. In 1967 he was released from prison and quickly formed the "Family," and on August 8 and 9, 1969, orchestrated the notorious Tate–LaBianca murders. On March 29, 1971, Manson and three other Family members were sentenced to death. They were all spared the death penalty and Manson went on to become a cultural icon and the subject of numerous books, articles, documentaries and movies. He died of natural causes in 2017, having been incarcerated for almost half a century.

12.1 The last known inmate ID prison badge worn by Charles Manson before his death. Interestingly, his DOB is given as 11 November, not 12 as is widely recorded. Inmates had to carry these on their person at all times, meaning this badge was worn by Manson for several years. The badge was obtained from a close associate of Manson's, who had received it after his death.

12.2 The cremains of Charles Manson were distributed to those close to Jason Freeman, Manson's grandson. In addition to the cremains are the announcement card and a flower that was part of the funeral arrangement that sat on top of his casket [this can be seen on page 26].

12.3 A Martin DS-16 LSH guitar sent to Corcoran State Prison with the Martin name filed off, since the guitar's value exceeded the gift limit of $250. Manson's Nordic-style script can be seen etched into the headstock with the symbols "Man" and "Sun." His blood appears inside the guitar, where he cut his finger changing the strings. After obtaining the instrument, the collector spoke to Manson, who explained the reason behind the etching of the "wolf paws," saying 'My followers were often given wolf names."

12.3

13.1

13. Deadlier Than the Male

Crime statisticians report that men account for almost 90 percent of the world's homicides and, according to research carried out by Radford and Florida Gulf Coast Universities, women only account for around 7 percent of serial killer activity in the last 40 years.

Aileen Wuornos was a tortured soul her entire life. The child of two severely dysfunctional teenage parents and the victim of childhood sexual abuse, she grew into a "monster." Although not the most prolific, with "only" seven murders, she won the sympathy and compassion of many along with the interest of Hollywood, with countless books, TV shows, and movies documenting how and why she did what she did.

13.1 The L.A. Gear sneakers Aileen Wuornos was wearing at the time of her arrest on January 9, 1991, at the Last Resort biker bar in Port Orange, Florida. Aileen signed both sneakers; she also scribbled: "Shoes I was busted in on 1-9-91."

13.2 A silver crucifix worn by Wuornos during her trial. She can be seen wearing this necklace in numerous photos, and it symbolized how close to Christ she had grown. Wuornos was devout during her incarceration and considered religion to be a priority in daily life.

13.3 A personally worn bandanna, the flip-flops she wore to the death chamber, and Aileen's final photo before she was executed. Prisoners are rarely photographed in handcuffs and leg irons; however, this was protocol when an inmate was due to be executed the following day. The photo is dated October 8, 2002. The State of Florida executed Aileen on October 9.

'Aileen signed both sneakers; she also scribbled: Shoes I was busted in on 1-9-91.'

Funeral Songs

Hands to Heaven - Breathe
Cigerrette in the Rain - Randy Crawford
Holding back the years - Simply Red
Rainy Night in Georgia - Randy Crawford
Yo Moo be there - Micheal Donald -
        Keiths favorite
Jesus is just alright - Dobbie Brothers
        Keiths favorite
Caroline - Concrete Blind
Bridge Over troubled Waters - Simon + Gar
Come Sail Away - Sticks - James Young
New Years Day - U2
Brown eyed girl - Van Morrison
My love is Alive - Gary Right
"Faithfull Leo" - Journey   Highway Ran
You Belong to the City - Glen frey.
I know I'm loosein you - Rare Earth
Love will keep us Alive -
Cant fight this feelin REO Speedwagon
              (my favorite group)

Natalie Merchant

DRESSED TO KILL

Hanging on a rack in a local department store, a sweater can be seen as nothing more than an innocuous piece of everyday clothing. But a sweater worn by Aileen Wuornos gives an insight into the psychological and physical torture she put herself through while on death row. As well as believing the guards were going to steal her eyeballs post mortem, Wuornos was convinced that they were perpetually trying to make her sick by keeping her cell exceptionally cold (an accusation the guards always denied). She wore the same sweater almost every day to try and stay warm.

Male inmate clothing, female inmate clothing, and female clothing worn by male inmates. The collection of Brandy Williamson focuses on garments worn by notorious killers, such as the cap of a murderous necrophiliac, the boxer shorts of a serial rapist who killed five of his victims, and the sweatpants worn by Charles Manson while incarcerated at California State Prison, Corcoran. Nothing could be considered more "everyday" than a pair of sneakers—unless they belonged to killer Joseph Druce, in which case they represent 48 years of pain, anger, and ultimately revenge.

Understanding the desire to possess an article once owned by a serial killer is complex. Many experts in the field of psychology say the seeking out of clothing worn by deviants of society sends us further down a labyrinth of potential psychological motivations. Brandy explains her own interest: "I don't collect it to glorify killers or out of some sick fascination with murder and death. I do find it fascinating that I can physically connect myself to some of the worst people on the planet by holding a pair of underwear that was worn by someone on death row. It is an interesting experience. And to be honest, some of the artwork to come from these folks is really good! People like Glen Rogers, Chuck Reinhardt, Keith Jesperson ... they're all pretty talented fellas."

"I don't care for school-shooter items, although I've got a few Columbine shirts. Lately, I've been more interested in finding more Jack Kevorkian items. I own one of his artwork prints, but I would love to have an original. My holy grail would probably be the original oil on canvas, 'Nearer My God to Thee,' by Kevorkian. Although, I'd settle for just a signed print!"

The collection of Brandy Williamson

Although women make up a large part of the true crime fan base, the field of true crime collecting is disproportionately male dominated. Brandy is one of the few female true crime collectors, and although she has not been in the game long, she has already curated an impressive collection of dark artifacts. "Although I'm new to true crime, I have been collecting oddities for years. Taxidermy, skulls, medical antiques, stuff like that, and it was here, in the oddities community, that I became aware of a market for true crime items."

As a child Brandy had a fascination with true crime and by the time she reached high school she was ready to take the plunge. Fascinated by the Tate–LaBianca murders, she wanted to write to the imprisoned Charles Manson. However, her mother feared that someone from the Family would come after her and forbade her from reaching out. Brandy settled for writing her senior leadership essay on Manson.

"The first item I ever purchased was artwork by Charles Manson. Since then, I have acquired some other great pieces, with a concentration on artwork and inmate-worn clothing. In fact, if I had to choose my favorite true crime possession, it would be a toss-up between my Charles Manson sweatpants and my Aileen Wuornos underwear and bra set."

Photos by Kyle Jarrad

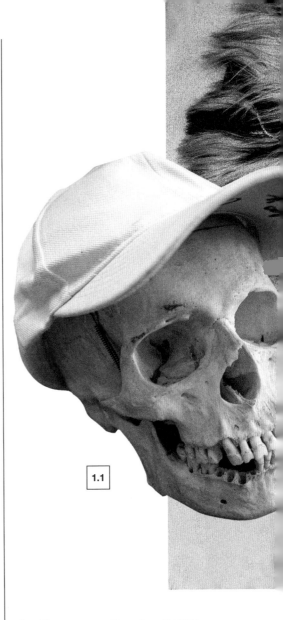

1.1

1. Sunset Strip Killers

Doug Clark was one half of the duo known as the Sunset Strip Killers. Between June 1 and August 1980, Clark and his partner Carol Bundy were allegedly involved in at least seven incidents of rape, murder, decapitation, and necrophilia. Clark was convicted and sentenced to death in 1983. However, many believe that he was innocent and did not get a fair trial.

1.1 A hat owned by Doug Clark while serving his sentence on death row, where, as of 2021, he remains in California's notorious San Quentin State Prison.

2. Manson Style

In December 1969, Charles Manson and four other Family members were indicted on murder and conspiracy charges in the Tate–La Bianca killings. For the next 225 days, Manson and the Family appeared almost daily on the front page of newspapers and magazines, and on countless TV news reports.

Criminologists and psychologists have credited Manson's hairstyle and the clothes he wore as being influential in his ability to lull his followers into a state of complacency: he looked and dressed like them, and his hair and beard resembled that of Jesus (symbolizing love and peace). His style also made people view him as a man of power and intimidation, often combining flower power clothes with army fatigues and camouflage gear.

2.1 **A pair of sweatpants worn by Charles Manson, given to a pen pal while Manson was "in the hole" for a rule violation.**

3.1

3. Seven Counts of Murder

Todd Kohlhepp began his killing in 2003, when he was 42 years old, but his troubles began much earlier, and he was described as a troublesome child as early as nursery school.

In 1987 Kohlhepp was sentenced to 15 years for kidnapping and raping a 15-year-old girl. While in prison he studied for an undergraduate degree, and on release in 2001 he started and developed a successful real-estate business. Nevertheless, Kohlhepp gained a reputation for being abusive and creepy. Between 2003 and 2016 he killed seven men and women. On May 26, 2017, he pleaded guilty to the seven counts of murder and was sentenced to seven consecutive life sentences without the possibility of parole.

3.1 **Gun case, blanket, and gloves purchased at the estate auction of Todd Kohlhepp. A first aid kit and zip ties were found inside the gun case.**

'Kohlhepp gained
a reputation for being
abusive and creepy.
Between 2003 and
2016 he killed seven
men and women.'

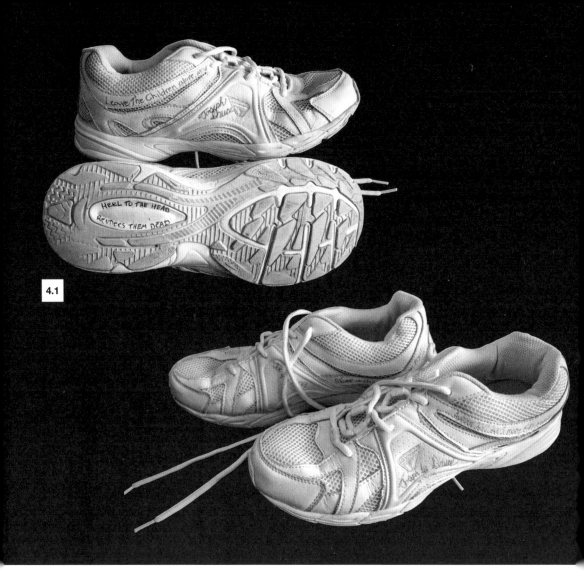

4. Heel to the Head Renders Them Dead

As a child, life was a nightmare for Joseph Druce. Allegedly, he was severely beaten by his father and from the age of eight sexually abused by three men, including a neighbor and a man with a religious affiliation.

While hitchhiking in 1988, Druce was picked up by the 51-year-old George Rollo. According to Druce, Rollo tried to rub his groin. Druce reacted violently, beating Rollo and throwing him in the trunk of the car, later strangling him. Druce was quickly arrested and held on a first-degree murder charge. The defense presented a case highlighting that Druce had been in psychiatric treatment since he was five years old. This did little to dissuade the judge and jury, and he was sentenced to life in prison.

On the morning of August 23, 2003, as inmates were returning from lunch in the protective custody unit at Souza-Baranowski Correctional Center, Druce allegedly slipped into the cell of John J. Geoghan, a former Roman Catholic priest and convicted pedophile serving a ten-year sentence. Druce bound, strangled, and stomped Geoghan to death.

4.1 **Sneakers worn and signed by Joseph Druce. On the heel of the foot he allegedly used to stomp Geoghan to death, he has written: "Heel to the Head Renders Them Dead."**

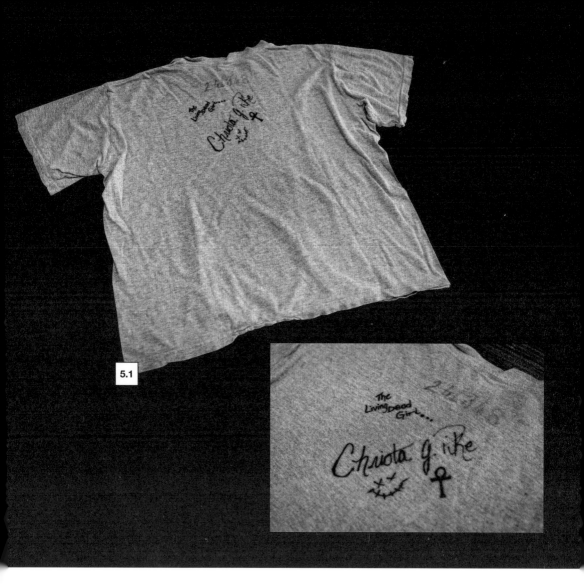

5. The Living Dead Girl

On March 30, 1996, 20-year-old Christa Pike received the dubious honor of being one of the youngest women to be sentenced to death in the United States. Aged 18, while undertaking a vocational training program at the University of Tennessee, she murdered classmate Colleen Slemmer, who she thought was trying to steal her boyfriend. She tortured the girl with a box cutter, carving images into her chest before smashing her head in with a slab of asphalt. The asphalt shattered the victim's skull.

Pike kept a fragment of skull and began showing it to people around campus. Within 36 hours she and her two accomplices were arrested. Only Pike received a death sentence for the crime, and she is presently awaiting execution on death row in Tennessee Prison for Women.

5.1 A shirt owned and signed by Christa Pike while on death row. The shirt was sent to a pen pal.

'One of the youngest women to be sentenced to death in the United States.'

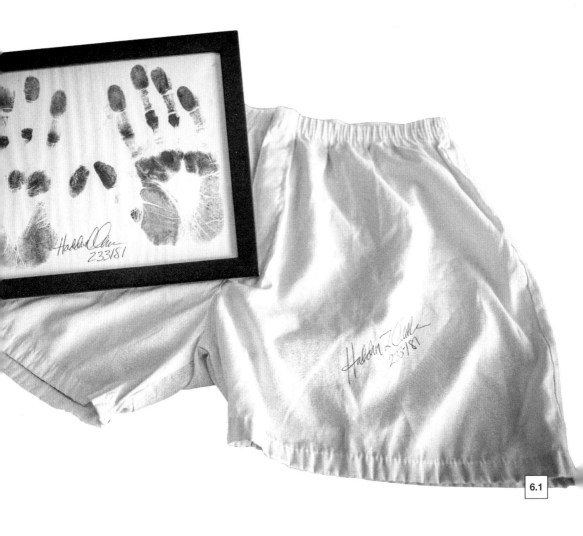

6.1

6. Cross-dressing Killer

"I buried one girl by the rocks in front of the castle," Hadden Clark admitted during a phone interview from the Maryland prison where he is serving his life sentence. However, it wasn't Clark speaking about his sordid past, but rather his alter ego, "Kristen Bluefin." It was under the persona of Bluefin that Clark confessed to a fellow inmate (who he believed was Jesus Christ) that he had killed at least a dozen women or girls.

In June 1993 Clark pleaded guilty to second-degree murder and was sentenced to 30 years in prison. In 1999 he was convicted of murdering a second person, adding another 30 years to his sentence.

6.1 Hadden Clark's handprints, along with a pair of boxer shorts worn and signed by Clark and given to one of his pen pals to be sold for commissary money.

6.2 These ladies' panties were purchased for Clark by the FBI for his trip to Cape Cod in 2000 to search for one of the bodies he had hidden. Clark insisted his alter ego, Kristen Bluefin, go on the search, hence the FBI's purchase of underwear, a skirt, and a blouse for him to wear.

Dressed to Kill

6.2

Funeral Songs
Hands to Heaven - Breathe
Cigarette in the Rain - Randy Crawford
Holding back the years - Simply Red
Rainy Night in Georgia - Randy Crawford
Yo nos ba there - Micheal Donald -
Jesus is just alright - Dobbie Brothers
                    Keiths favorite
Caroline - Concrete Blind
Bridge Over troubled Waters - Simon + Her
Come Sail away - Sticks - James Young
New Years Day - U2
Brown eyed girl - Van Morrison
My love is alive - Gary Right
"Faithfull Leo" - Journey (Highway Ra
you belong to the city - Glen fry -
I know I'm loosein you - Rare Earth
Love will keep us alive -
cant fight this feelin REO Speedwago
                    (my favorite group)

Natalie Merchant

7. Steal Her Eyeballs

Using the Psychopathy Checklist, Aileen Wuornos was found to have a psychopathic personality with a PCL-R score of 32, the cutoff score for psychopathy in the United States being 30.

While Aileen was serving time on death row after confessing to the murder of seven men, her psychotic behavior and paranoia continued. Aileen was convinced guards would steal her belongings after she was executed. She even thought they would steal her eyeballs. Aileen wanted her childhood friend, Dawn Botkins, to have all her belongings after execution, and asked Dawn to view her body as soon as possible to make sure her eyes were still there.

7.1 A necklace worn by Aileen while on death row, and given to Dawn when Wuornos was executed. Dawn kept this hidden until Brandy purchased it from her in 2019. Also shown are Aileen's watch, a childhood photo, prison snapshots and a list of funeral songs she compiled.

7.2 A complete set of religious comics that Aileen owned. Many of them have her notes written in the margins.

7.2

'Aileen was convinced
guards would steal her
belongings after she
was executed. She even
thought they would
steal her eyeballs.'

7.4

WUORNOS-A
AI50924

7.3 A sweater owned by Aileen Wuornos on death row. Aileen was always cold and wore this red sweater almost every day. Dawn said that Aileen thought the guards were tormenting her and would keep her cell colder than anyone else's.

7.4 A tag from Wuornos's death row jumpsuit. Aileen mailed it to Dawn toward the end of her sentence. Dawn said it was one of the most surprising items Aileen ever sent her, and she was amazed it wasn't found and confiscated.

7.5 A sweatshirt and bandanna worn by Wuornos while on death row. The bandanna is still tied in the same spot as when Dawn received it after Aileen's execution.

7.6 One of the last sets of underwear owned by Aileen Wuornos. She made sure to leave every personal belonging to Dawn, and told Dawn to sell the underwear when she needed to make a mortgage payment.

Dressed to Kill

7.6

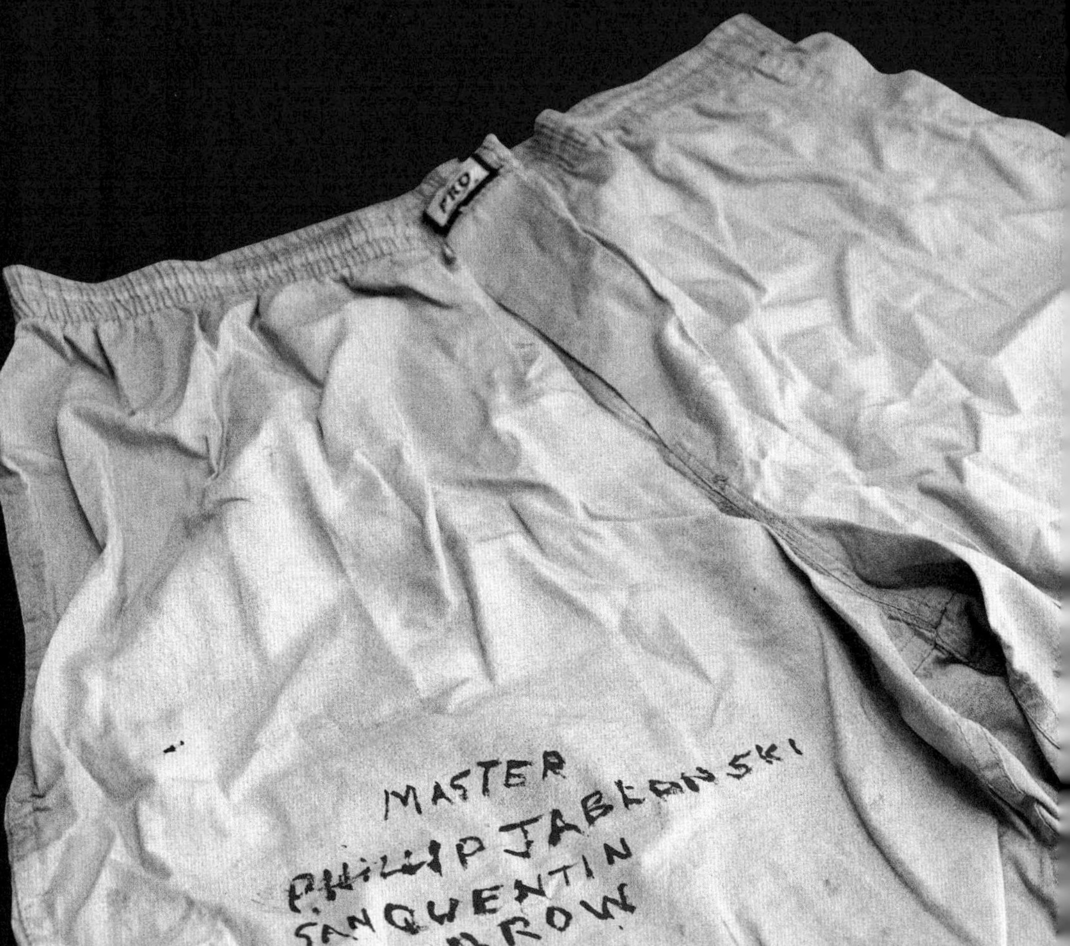

8.1

8. Remorseless Predator

Phillip Carl Jablonski was born in Joshua Tree, California, in 1946. He left in 1966 to join the Army and was discharged on medical grounds in 1969, having been diagnosed with a schizophrenic illness. On his return to the United States he ended up in Texas, and it was there that Jablonski began his career as a serial rapist and ultimately a serial killer.

By April 1991, he had raped countless women and killed five, including the rape, murder, and mutilation of a 38-year-old mother of two teenage girls. The mother was found lying dead and naked in the Colorado desert with the words "I Love Jesus" carved into her back and her eyes and ears removed.

That same year Jablonski was arrested, found guilty of five murders, including those of two of his ex-wives and his former mother-in-law, and sentenced to death. He died in his cell in San Quentin State Prison on December 27, 2019, at the age of 73.

8.1 A pair of boxer shorts once owned by Phillip Jablonski while on death row. There are smudges of paint on them, which means he likely made many of his paintings in just his underwear.

'The mother was found lying dead and naked in the Colorado desert with the words "I Love Jesus" carved into her back'

Sharon Tate 1943 - 1969

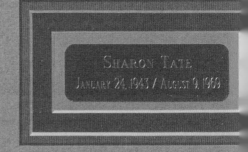

SHARON TATE
JANUARY 24, 1943 / AUGUST 9, 1969

A GALLERY OF FEAR

Hollywood's portrayal of serial killers usually includes them wanting to take a souvenir from their victim, anything from a piece of jewelry to a body part. They also have a tendency to return to the scene of the crime to revisit the body, sometimes to engage in a sexual act, either masturbation or necrophilia. Both these characteristics are accurate. However, when these killers are eventually locked up, their ability to revisit is no longer possible, though the desire remains.

Some of the more depraved killers who are on death row or serving out a life sentence have resorted to drawing images of their victims, at times in the complimentary style of a portrait, at other times in "compromising positions." Psychologists believe this is a way for the killers to relive their crimes and keep their murderous legacy alive.

Casey Tillman's collection includes examples of this heinous behavior by the killers Sam Little and Gerard Schaefer, along with a blood-curdling and very rare piece in the same vein by Dennis Rader, the "BTK Killer." Casey says: "I enjoy studying specific cases and owning a personal object from the person or persons involved. When I come into possession of a killer's letter or artwork, I instinctively try to psychologically profile the person by deciphering or decoding the letter or artwork to understand why they've committed the atrocities they have been accused and found guilty of. Find out what makes these folks tick."

"Owning a nineteenth-century Lizzie Borden signed document or a John Wayne Gacy oil painting is historic ... yes, a dark and somber part of history, but history nonetheless. And although I look at my collection as representative of a specific segment of history, I respect that others may find some of the items offensive. To those who say true crime collecting is immoral, I ask them, why is it when you see items similar to these in a museum you are not offended?"

The collection of Casey Tillman

Although Casey didn't become drawn into the true crime collecting scene until 2016, his obsession with the dark side began at the tender age of eight: "I've always had a fascination with 'scary' movies. I grew up watching '80s and '90s horror films. Being so young, I didn't fully comprehend the storylines; however, I have to admit I was mesmerized by the violence and gore."

In his twenties Casey began collecting horror movie memorabilia. Then, in 2016, he received a message asking if he would be interested in purchasing a letter written by Edward Spreitzer. Casey had no idea who this was, but discovered that Spreitzer was part of the Chicago Ripper Crew, a satanic cult and crime organization composed of serial killers, cannibals, rapists, and necrophiles.

Casey purchased the Spreitzer letter, and was fascinated by Edward's perfectly spaced typewriter-style handwriting. He says that, although the content was relatively dull, he seemed to be a pleasant person. However, he knew from his case record that this guy was a ruthless killer, a "real-life monster." He couldn't believe he was holding a handwritten letter from a serial killer: "I believe that was the moment I decided to become a serious collector of true crime."

Photos by Dan Howell

1.1

1. Coast-to-Coast Killer

No amount of dysfunctional and/or abusive family life experienced as a child can justify the abhorrent behavior of Tommy Lynn Sells. It didn't matter whether you were a man, woman, or child. In fact, women, children, and people who showed kindness toward this monster were his favorite victims.

Sells was not satisfied with just killing but went out of his way to be exceptionally brutal. Arrested on January 2, 2000, for the murder of 13-year-old Kaylene Harris, Sells was found guilty and sentenced to death. Police believed he was responsible for another 22 killings, but during a death interview with forensic psychiatrist Dr. Michael Stone, Sells confessed to over 70 other murders. He was eventually executed via lethal injection on April 3, 2014.

1.1 | Demonic skull painting by Tommy Sells, possibly intended as a self-portrait.

ISSEI SAGAWA
DEAD MANS HAND

2. The Kobe Cannibal

Issei Sagawa is a Japanese murderer, cannibal, and necrophile who exhibited all of that deviant behavior in the killing of Dutch woman Renée Hartevelt in Paris. On June 11, 1981, Sagawa invited Hartevelt, his classmate at the Sorbonne, to dinner at his apartment. Once there, Sagawa shot Hartevelt in the neck and over the next few days carried out necrophilic acts and consumed various body parts. He ate her breasts and face, saving other parts in his refrigerator.

French authorities arrested Sagawa as he attempted to toss suitcases stuffed with Hartevelt's body parts into a lake. Determined to be legally insane and unfit to stand trial by the French judge, Sagawa was ruled to be held indefinitely in a mental institution. Japanese media coverage of Sagawa turned him into a bizarre, macabre celebrity. Sagawa was deported to Japan, where he was immediately committed to Matsuzawa Hospital in Tokyo.

Matsuzawa psychologists all declared him to be sane. However, since French authorities had ruled Sagawa's mental state to be unfit and the charges against him in France had been dropped, he could not be detained in Japan. He was able to check himself out of the hospital on August 12, 1986, and has subsequently remained free.

2.1 **Despite Sagawa being found sane, his artwork may paint a different picture of his mental state.**

'French authorities arrested Sagawa as he attempted to toss suitcases stuffed with Hartevelt's body parts into a lake.'

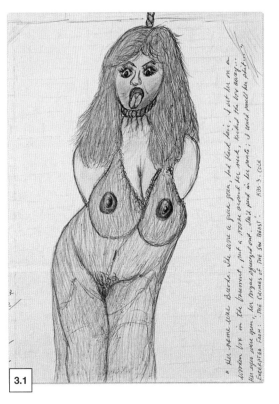

3.1

4.1

3. Priest, Teacher, Policeman

Gerard Schaefer had a troubled childhood and was a sexually deviant teen. As a young man, he decided he wanted to be either a priest, a teacher, or a policeman. He was rejected from a seminary and fired as a teacher, but was hired by the small-town Wilton Manors Police Department even though he failed the psychological exam.

After a few years on the job, Schaefer was fired for kidnapping two girls and tying them to a tree "to teach them a lesson." In November 1972 he was tried, and in January 1973 sentenced to a year in jail. He was never released because, while serving that one year, he was implicated in the 1972 torture, rape, and murder of two young girls.

On December 3, 1995, Vincent Rivera, another inmate, muscled his way into Schaefer's cell. Rivera slashed Schaefer's throat and stabbed him in both eyes.

3.1 Schaefer drawing entitled "The Hangman," with disturbing annotations that clearly demonstrate his twisted, sadistic, and murderous objectification of women and his victims.

4. Thirteen

The number of victims attributable to the heinous behavior of so many serial killers is hard to verify, and the case of Arthur Shawcross, "the Genesee River Killer," is no exception. In 1972 Shawcross killed one, or possibly two children and served 14 years of a 25-year sentence. After lying low for two years on his release, between 1988 and 1989 Shawcross went on a killing spree murdering sex workers.

Most people believe the accurate number of his victims is between 12 and 14. Based on the numeral Shawcross has placed within his painting of the grim reaper, 13 is apparently the number he has himself settled on.

4.1 A Shawcross reaper adorned with a red "13" and a bloody sickle.

5.1

5. The Crawl Space

Between December 22 and December 29, 1978, police recovered 27 bodies from John Wayne Gacy's property in Chicago, Illinois, 26 of them found buried in the crawl space beneath his front porch. An additional victim was found buried beneath the concrete floor of his garage.

After his arrest Gacy volunteered to help facilitate the search effort by sketching a layout of his basement to highlight where the corpses were buried. Gacy stated that he eventually lost count of how many young men were buried in his crawl space and had considered storing bodies in his attic before opting to dispose of them in the Des Plaines River. During his trial, Gacy joked that the only thing he was guilty of was "running a cemetery without a license."

'Gacy stated that he eventually lost count of how many young men were buried in his crawl space.'

5.1 Original 8×10" crime scene photo used as a trial exhibit with a stamped and embossed Cook County seal. The photo shows the location of the bodies of six young men.

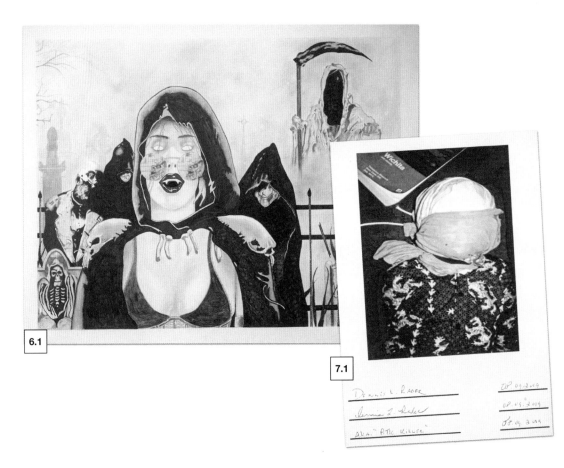

6.1

7.1

6. Strangler's Art

Between 1977 and 1979, Kenneth Bianchi and his cousin Angelo Buono Jr. kidnapped, tortured, brutally raped, and murdered ten women in California and Washington state. Although known as the Hillside Strangler murders, Bianchi and Buono experimented with other killing methods, such as lethal injection, electric shock, and poisoning.

Bianchi and Buono were picked out of a police lineup and arrested in January 1979. Bianchi was spared the death penalty and given life in prison with the possibility of parole. He will next be eligible for parole in 2025. Bianchi is also a suspect in the Alphabet murders, three unsolved murders in his home city of Rochester, New York, from 1971 to 1973.

6.1 | This large painting Bianchi made in prison, incorporating several dark themes, allows a peek into his sick mind.

7. BTK Signs His Work

As despicable people go, Dennis Rader, also known as BTK (an abbreviation he gave himself for "bind, torture, kill"), is by far one of the most deplorable. Known in his community as polite and well mannered, between 1974 and 1991 Rader brutally murdered ten people in Kansas, including children. He sent taunting letters to the police and newspapers describing the details of his crimes.

On January 19, 1991, Rader claimed his tenth victim, Dolores Davis. After over a decade of lying low, Rader resumed sending letters in 2004, which led to his arrest in 2005 and a subsequent guilty plea. Rader is serving ten consecutive life sentences at El Dorado Correctional Facility.

7.1 | An anonymous "friend" of Rader's snuck in copies of the police evidence photos from his slaughter of members of the Otero family in 1974, and Rader signed and dated the copies. He is clearly remorseless.

8.1

8. Sharon Tate Murder

On the night of August 8, 1969, following Charles Manson's instructions, Tex Watson drove Susan Atkins, Linda Kasabian, and Patricia Krenwinkel to "that house where Melcher used to live," to "totally destroy" everyone in it and to do it "as gruesome as you can." A small get-together at the house at 10050 Cielo Drive that evening included the home's owner, movie actress Sharon Tate, wife of film director Roman Polanski. Tate was eight-and-a-half-months pregnant.

The gruesome details of the murders are well documented, with all occupants suffering a bloody death by multiple stabbings. Tate pleaded to be allowed to live long enough to give birth, but Atkins and Watson stabbed her 16 times, killing her. Manson had told the women to "leave a sign—something witchy," so Atkins wrote "pig" on the front door in Sharon Tate's blood.

'Manson had told the women to "leave a sign—something witchy," so Atkins wrote "pig" on the front door in Sharon Tate's blood.'

8.1 **Signature of Sharon Tate. Despite Tate's popularity, examples of her signature are scarce due to her short life.**

Dividend October 6 1890. $2.50 per Share.

Name	Location	Shares	Amount	Date	Remarks
Adams Lydian S.	Fall River	3	7 50	Oct 9	Lydian S. Adams
Adams Robert	Fall River	4	10 00	Oct 9	Robert Adams by L.S.A.
Aiken Minerva E.	Freetown	5	12 50	Oct 6	G.H Hathaway for order
Alden Mary M.	Berkley	5	12 50	Oct 6	G.H Hathaway for order
Allen Mary A.	Berkley	2	5 00	Oct 6	Remitted Mary A. Allen
Allen George S.	Fall River	3	7 50	Oct 20	George S Allen
Almy Annie E.	Tiverton	1	2 50	Oct 24	Annie E. Almy.
Anthony David & others Trustee	Fall River	25	62 50	Oct 11	E.S Thayer, Trustee
Anthony Elizabeth M.	Fall River	12	30 00	Oct 30	Elizabeth M. Anthony
Anthony Lauretta R.W.	Fall River	11	27 50	Oct	L.R Anthony
Anthony Mary B.	Providence	10	25 00	Oct 14	Remitted Mary B Anthony
Ashley Joannah H.	Fall River	7	17 50	Oct 17	Wm H Ashley for order
Babbitt George R.	Providence	2	5 00	Oct 25	Geo R Babbitt
Baptist Society Six Principle	Newport	20	50 00	Oct 6	Remitted Newport Nat Bank
Barrows Davis J.	Freetown	10	25 00	Oct 6	B G Porter per order
Bateman Julia A.	Fall River	12	30 00	Oct 6	Chas B Leuther
Bishop Zephaniah C.	Attleboro	20	50 00	Oct 3 1891	Remitted Zephaniah C Bishop
Blaisdell Annie W.	Fall River	16	40 00	Nov 10	Annie W. Blaisdell.
Blake Mercy T.	Taunton	3	7 50	Dec 17 1892	Paid Metacomet Nat Bank under release of Nov 20/92
Blevins Mary M.	Fall River	5	12 50	Oct 9	Mary M. Blevins
Borden Abner D.	Fall River	10	25 00	Oct 6	Abner D Borden
Borden Abbie L.	Fall River	10	25 00	Oct 6	Abbie L Borden by A Borden
Borden Caroline	Boston	6	15 00	Oct 6	Cr to A/c Caroline Borden
Borden Emma L.	Fall River	2	5 00	Oct 16	Emma L. Borden
Borden Jerome C. Trustee for Maria Grace	Fall River	2	5 00	Apr 14	Jerome C Borden Tr
Borden Lizzie A.	Fall River	2	5 00	Nov 4	Lizzie A. Borden
Borden Lydia Ann	Fall River	10	25 00	Nov 4	Lydia A Borden
Borden Mary Ann	Fall River	14	35 00	Oct 7	Andrew J Borden Atty
Borden Philip H.	Fall River	10	25 00	Oct 8	Philip H Borden by S.S.B
Borden Richard P.	Fall River	10	25 00	Oct 6	R B Borden
Bourne Standish Trustee	New Bedford	6	15 00	Oct 6	Remitted Standish Bourne Trustee
Bowen Sarah S.	Newport	25	62 50	Oct 7	Remitted Sarah S. Bowen
Brayton Benjamin	Bristol	5	12 50	Oct 17	B Brayton
	Forward	288	720 00		

9.1

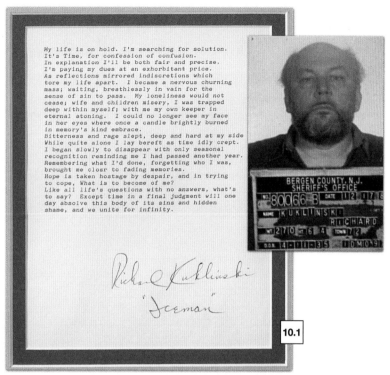

My life is on hold. I'm searching for solution.
It's Time, for confession of confusion.
In explanation I'll be both fair and precise.
I'm paying my dues at an exhorbitant price.
As reflections mirrored indiscretions which
tore my life apart. I became a nervous churning
mass; waiting, breathlessly in vain for the
sense of sin to pass. My loneliness would not
cease; wife and children misery, I was trapped
deep within myself; with me my own keeper in
eternal atoning. I could no longer see my face
in her eyes where once a candle brightly burned
in memory's kind embrace.
Bitterness and rage slept, deep and hard at my side
While quite alone I lay bereft as time idly crept.
I began slowly to disappear with only seasonal
recognition reminding me I had passed another year.
Remembering what I'd done, forgetting who I was,
brought me closr to fading memories.
Hope is taken hostage by despair, and in trying
to cope, What is to become of me?
Like all life's questions with no answers, what's
to say? Except time in a final judgment will one
day absolve this body of its sins and hidden
shame, and we unite for infinity.

10.1

9. Lizzie Borden

August 4, 1892, was shaping up to be a warm summer's day when Abby and Andrew Borden were found hacked to death in their home at Fall River, Massachusetts. The attack was so brutal that Andrew's face was nearly split in two and one of his eyeballs cut in half. Abby's skull was smashed to pieces. Despite the 81 whacks suggested in the lyrics of the famous poem, the Bordens were killed by a total of 29 strikes of an ax. It would become one of the most famous cases in American criminal history.

Suspicion soon fell on one of the Bordens' two daughters, Lizzie. She was brought in for questioning, where she gave conflicting alibis, and two days later she was arrested. The trial was sensationalized, and at one point the prosecuting attorney tossed the actual severed heads of Andrew and Abby Borden onto the courtroom table. Despite substantial circumstantial evidence, Lizzie was found innocent.

9.1 This rare Borden artifact is a dividend sheet from 1890 and includes the signatures of Abby, Emma, and Lizzie Borden.

10. The Iceman

In 1988 Richard "the Iceman" Kuklinski was sentenced to life in prison for the murder of four underworld associates. He later confessed to somewhere over 200 killings, alleging that most of his gruesome murders were commissioned mob hits, including those on Carmine Galante and Roy DeMeo. He also identified himself as one of the shooters in John Gotti's hit on Paul Castellano. To many inside the criminal world, Kuklinski was referred to as "the one-man army."

Kuklinski said he used a variety of methods to kill, including guns, knives, explosives, tire irons, fire, poison, asphyxiation, feeding people to cave rats, and even bare-handed beatings "just for the exercise." Many of the killings Kuklinski takes credit for are disputed by law enforcement and fellow underworld figures. However, even if he is only responsible for half the murders he claims, it still makes him an "Iceman."

10.1 Prison Polaroids of Kuklinski, along with a poem written by him that expresses a rare sensitive side of the killer. Although it implies remorse for the pain his actions have caused him and his own family, it shows no remorse for his victims and their families.

11. No Remorse

With the FBI confirming that evidence links Sam Little to 60 murders, and Little himself confessing to killing 93, an FBI report describes him as "possibly the most prolific serial killer in U.S. history." Apprehended on September 5, 2012, and given four life sentences without the possibility of parole, Little showed no reluctance in boasting about his kills and took to making sketches of victims. To add further insult to the grisly deaths suffered by these women, 40 of the 50 confirmed murder victims are only identified as unnamed black or white females.

11.1 **The first page of this letter is Little being "romantic." He writes that if he was out of prison, "I would make you be mine, and I would love you the way I love my women. Keep that in mind, and don't put words in my mouth." The second page includes a disturbing account of one of his 1984 murders, saying his victim liked what he did until she wanted to breathe, and when he was done she looked like a dead angel, with no scars or bruises. He referred to his victims as "sisters." He also painted a picture of his unnamed 1984 Kentucky sister/victim.**

'Possibly the most prolific serial killer in U.S. history.'

I am sorry I wrote all this shit so dont
get to sleep HA HA. STAY STRONG AND
REAL YOUR MAN SAM FOR EVER

LOVE
SAM

PS, they Both money ORDERS goT here   good Looking
out. YOUR MAN, SAM (HAHA)

YOUR SISTER LAST PicTure WAS LIKE YOU A
FReAK, BuT She Love ORTHer Choco LATE BARS
So I goT my nuTS off HER AND TOOK HER OUT
FOR EVER So LIKED IT TILL She WAWTED TO
BREATH She Looked LIKE A dEAD ANGLE NO
SCARS or BRUCES   NOW YOU KNOW

~~YOU RED PRObLEY WANTS~~
~~to SELL THIS~~

PS; YOUR MY WIFE I CAN
TALK TO YOU LIKE MY
WIFE HA HA HA HA HA

LOVE

LITTLE
8/23/19

YOUR SISTER
FOUND IN
MONTERY
1989

11.1

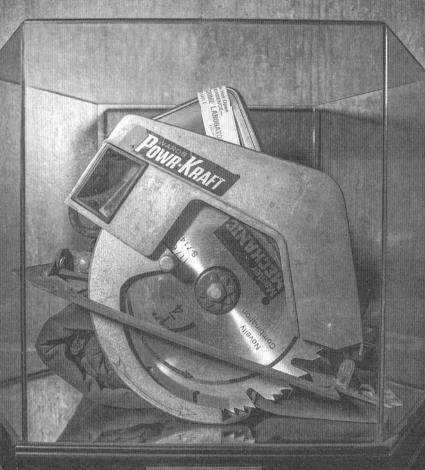

ROBERT BERDELLA
THE KANSAS CITY BUTCHER
SKILSAW

A PREFERENCE FOR 'TOP SHELF' KILLERS

Experts involved in the case of Robert Berdella testified that he was one of the most brutal serial killers ever; however, Berdella never gained the infamy of monsters like Dahmer and Bundy. That may be because his body count was a "mere" six, but what he lacked in quantity he made up for in sheer viciousness.

Berdella was an American serial killer—dubbed "the Kansas City Butcher" and "the Collector" by the press—who kidnapped, raped, and tortured his victims. He was convicted of killing at least six men between 1984 and 1987 in Kansas City, Missouri, after forcing his victims to endure periods of torture lasting up to six weeks.

Death came slowly and painfully to the young men who found themselves bound and gagged on Berdella's filthy bed. The Kansas City Butcher lived up to his moniker, with a penchant for injecting his victims' throats with Drano so they could no longer scream, pouring bleach into their eyes just to witness what would happen, sending jolts of electricity into their testicles, and ramming objects into their rectums so hard it would cause hemorrhaging.

Collector Devin Shomper says that for the last few years he has been obsessed with Berdella and his crimes. "My prized possession is an original self-portrait painting by him. Berdella used dog collars on his victims, and I am looking to purchase one of those taken into evidence from his home after his arrest." Devin's collection reads like a novel based on a series of heinous true-life crimes, with a cast of characters comprising "top shelf" real-life serial killers. "My primary concentration is crime memorabilia. I find certain crime cases historically significant and seek items from those events. It's fascinating to hold something that in some way is connected to a high-profile crime."

The juxtaposition of a Happy Face banner and Richard Ramirez's satanic ritual book have more in common than one would ever imagine or care to. The sadness of a missing person poster only goes deeper into a macabre world when it's discovered who drew the pencil sketch of a smiling girl that sits beside the poster. The "beauty" of true crime collecting is that all is not what it first appears to be.

The collection of Devin Shomper

Devin's first piece of memorabilia was an original letter handwritten and signed by controversial rock star GG Allin, along with its envelope, adorned with a GG original drawing. Allin is a figure the true crime community has embraced, not for his criminal record, which only constituted misdemeanors, but for his well-documented antisocial behavior on stage and off. The first official serial killer piece bought by Devin was a signed John Wayne Gacy letter, also with its envelope.

Devin collects true crime artifacts alongside other categories, such as items related to the paranormal. He owns a very rare original "Frank's Box," also known as a "Ghost Box," which is a device invented by the late Frank Sumption that scanned the AM radio band and allegedly could pick up spirit voices within the broadcasts. Devin also runs his own company that produces horror-themed costumes and props.

"I'm pretty selective about what I'll add to my collection. I have passed on plenty of true crime items offered to me; either it's overpriced, in my opinion, or I think it's a fake, or I don't know enough about the case to make it relevant in my collection. And I don't buy fingernails, toenails, earwax, penis tracings, things like that. I know it sounds crazy that some inmates even do this, but they do."

Photos by Rodney Montgomery

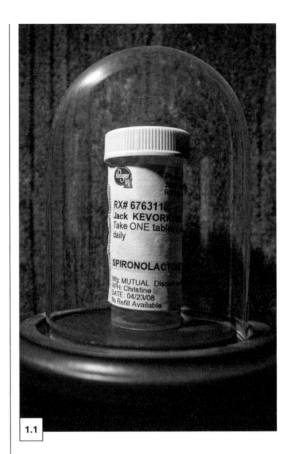

1.1

1. Dying is Not a Crime

Jack Kevorkian was an American pathologist. However, he is best known for being a proponent of euthanasia. He personally championed a terminal patient's right to die by physician-assisted suicide, saying, "Dying is not a crime."

Kevorkian stated that he assisted in the death of at least 130 patients. In November 1998, a videotape aired documenting the voluntary euthanasia of a man in the final stages of Lou Gehrig's disease. In the video Kevorkian himself administered the lethal injection, which proved to be highly significant since, previously, clients had reportedly completed the process themselves.

On March 26, 1999, Kevorkian was charged with second-degree murder and the delivery of a controlled substance. He was sentenced to 10 to 25 years in prison but was released on parole in June 2007 on condition he would not offer advice, participate in, or be present at the act of any suicide involving euthanasia.

1.1 | A prescription issued by Dr. Kevorkian a year after his release from prison.

2. The Happy Face Killer

At 6 foot 7½ inches and weighing approximately 240 pounds, Keith Hunter Jesperson is an imposing figure. He is convicted of murdering eight female victims and lays claim to having murdered 185 people—not the kind of person you would identify with a smiley face.

When a couple named Laverne Pavlinac and John Sosnovske falsely confessed to the murder of Jesperson's first victim, Taunja Bennett, and were convicted for the crime on February 8, 1991, Jesperson was infuriated by the attention they received. In response he wrote a confession on the bathroom wall of a truck stop 100 miles from the murder scene, signing it with a smiley face. Jesperson was arrested in March 1995 and is serving four life sentences at Oregon State Penitentiary.

2.1 This signed Jesperson smiley drawing is another example of a killer mocking both the public and his victims.

3. The Night Stalker

The subject of several films and a recent Netflix documentary series, Richard Ramirez terrorized LA in the 1980s with a killing spree that lasted over a year. Satanism and Ramirez go hand in hand. When carrying out his raping and killing spree he would have his victims profess their love of Satan while attacking them, or leave satanic symbols drawn on their lifeless bodies. He would eventually be convicted of 13 counts of murder, five counts of attempted murder, and 11 counts of sexual assault. When Ramirez appeared for his first court appearance on July 22, 1988, he raised a hand with a pentagram drawn on it and yelled, "Hail Satan!"

3.1 Richard Ramirez owned this satanic ritual book while he was in prison. The book was initially acquired from his wife, Doreen Ramirez, and includes a letter of authenticity from her.

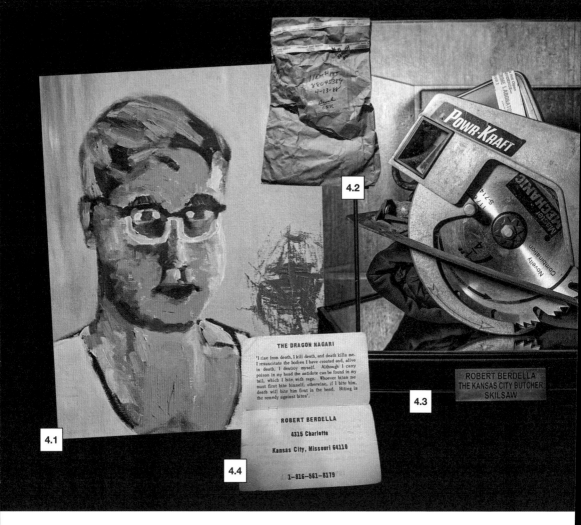

THE DRAGON NAGARI

'I rise from death, I kill death, and death kills me. I resuscitate the bodies I have created and, alive in death, I destroy myself. Although I carry poison in my head the antidote can be found in my tail, which I bite, with rage. Whoever bites me must first bite himself; otherwise, if I bite him, death will bite him first in the head. Biting is the remedy against bites'.

ROBERT BERDELLA

4315 Charlotte

Kansas City, Missouri 64110

1-816-561-8179

ROBERT BERDELLA
THE KANSAS CITY BUTCHER
SKILSAW

4. Darkest Fantasies

Between 1984 and 1987, Robert Berdella kidnapped, raped, tortured, and murdered at least six men in Kansas City, Missouri. On April 2, 1988, he was arrested and pleaded guilty to the first-degree murder of Larry Pearson. He would later admit to killing five more young men. The media christened him "the Kansas City Butcher" due to his practice of dissecting his victims with a circular saw, and then disposing of them in garbage bags. Upon capture and interrogation, Berdella described his murders as "some of my darkest fantasies becoming my reality."

4.1 | Rare example of a Robert Berdella self-portrait.

4.2 | Evidence bag that contained the electric circular saw.

4.3 | Electric circular saw taken as evidence from Berdella's home.

4.4 | While business cards from his well-known shop "Bob's Bazaar Bizarre" do pop up in collections, this rare business card was used to advertise the antiques he collected before opening the shop.

'The media christened him "the Kansas City Butcher" due to his practice of dissecting his victims with a circular saw'

5.1

6.1

5. Joel Rifkin's Jacket

Before Joel Rifkin went on to kill over a dozen women, predominantly sex workers, he was an outcast with learning disabilities, who did badly in school and was unpopular with classmates due to his poor social skills.

In 1989, killing Heidi Balch marked the beginning of his murderous ways. He dismembered her body, pulled out her teeth, cut off her fingertips, and put her head in a paint can that he left on a golf course in New Jersey. He left her legs in another part of New Jersey and dumped her torso and arms into the East River around New York City.

5.1   **A childhood jacket that belonged to Joel Rifkin and was originally acquired from his mother's attic. The jacket is stitched with "Joel" on the left chest area.**

6. Bundy's Bug

If you were a passenger in Ted Bundy's 1968 Volkswagen Bug, odds were that you would be semiconscious, handcuffed to the car's frame, and lying on the car floor, since the passenger seat had been taken out. You wouldn't be able to open the door, as the inside handle had also been removed.

Bundy's VW became an integral part of his killing: a place to strangle his victims, a vehicle to literally drive them to their death, its headlights used so that Bundy could better see his victims die as he squeezed the life from them. The car itself is now owned by the crime memorabilia collector Arthur Nash and is on display at the Alcatraz Museum.

6.1   **Rusted remnants from the 1968 Volkswagen Bug that Bundy used as an "accomplice" in his multiple murders.**

7.1

7.2

7. The Cannibal Cafe

Forty-year-old Armin Meiwes had always fantasized about eating human flesh, and in March 2001 he posted a classified ad on the now-defunct internet forum The Cannibal Cafe. He wrote that he was "looking for a normally built 18- to 25-year-old to be slaughtered and then consumed." An engineer from Berlin, Armando Brandes, agreed and showed up at Meiwes's Wüstefeld apartment.

Meiwes videotaped the entire evening. It began with Brandes swallowing 20 sleeping pills before Meiwes amputated Brandes's penis so that they could eat it together. Brandes tried to eat some of his own penis raw but could not, apparently claiming it was too "chewy."

Meiwes ran a warm bath, where Brandes lay bleeding as Meiwes read a *Star Trek* book.

Meiwes finally killed Brandes by stabbing him in the throat, then hung his body on a meat hook. He dismembered and ate the corpse over the next ten months, storing body parts in his freezer.

Meiwes was arrested in December 2002, when someone alerted authorities to new online advertisements for victims. Investigators searched his home and found Brandes's body parts and the videotape of the killing. In 2004, Meiwes was convicted of manslaughter and sentenced to eight-and-a-half years in prison, but two years later he was retried and given a life sentence.

7.1 **The grab bar from Meiwes's bathtub, seen in the crime-scene photo, where Armando Brandes was murdered.**

7.2 **A rusty saw taken as evidence from Meiwes's apartment.**

8. Born to Kill

Hadden Clark came from a volatile family. Both his parents were alcoholics; his mother dressed him in girls' clothes when intoxicated and his father eventually committed suicide. In 1984 Hadden's brother Bradfield became infamous when he killed a female coworker, cut up her body, barbecued her breasts, and ate them.

Not to be outdone, in 1986 Hadden killed a six-year-old girl and drank her blood, then on October 18, 1992, he killed a 23-year-old woman, Laura Houghteling. This was the murder that led to his arrest. Although Hadden was officially charged with only two murders, he claims to have killed dozens of people, starting as a teenager.

In December 2000, Hadden led the police to a property formerly owned by his grandparents. Here they uncovered a plastic bucket containing more than 200 pieces of jewelry. Among the items was Houghteling's high-school class ring. Clark claimed the pieces were "trophies" he took from his victims. All this jewelry lends credence to Hadden's claim that he murdered dozens.

8.1 A missing person poster, and a portrait drawn by Clark of his 23-year-old victim, Laura Houghteling.

'Although Hadden was officially charged with only two murders, he claims to have killed dozens of people'

9.1

9. Bind, Torture, Kill

Dennis Rader called himself the BTK Killer, standing for "bind, torture, kill." The key word here was "bind." Although there was no clear pattern to the ten murders he committed around Wichita, Kansas, between 1974 and 1991, there was a consistent piece of evidence: intricate knots used to bind his victims.

When Rader was taken into custody in 2005, he waived his right to an attorney, and in addition to confessing to his crimes he admitted to a fascination with bindings. Rader spoke of a time when, at eight years old, he saw his grandmother bind the legs of the Sunday dinner chicken and chop off its head, and this had aroused him.

During the interrogation, Rader also revealed to investigators where they could find evidence from his 17-year killing spree. Most of these items were found in his home, including Polaroids of Rader himself wearing clothing he took from his victims and in various states of bondage.

9.1 A chilling artifact from Dennis Rader: one of the ropes he used to bind his victims.

10. The Vampire of Paris

These various items belonged to Nico Claux (also a featured collector in this book, see page 126). A self-proclaimed Satanist and convicted murderer, Claux also robbed graves and committed acts of cannibalism while working at the Paris morgue in the mid-1990s. After serving just over seven years of a 12-year sentence, Claux was released in 2002 and is now an artist, writer, and "death merchant" who collaborates with other convicted murderers on art projects and trades in true crime memorabilia.

10.1 **Devin is in contact with Nico and asked him to comment on the pieces shown here. The artifacts include a "crucifix that I have used in black mass rituals," a "suit that I used to wear when I worked in the morgue of Jeanne Garnier hospice in Paris— I would also wear a tie worn by Richard Ramirez," and (rather ominously considering his cannibalistic predilections) a "knife and fork that I have used."**

A Preference for "Top Shelf" Killers

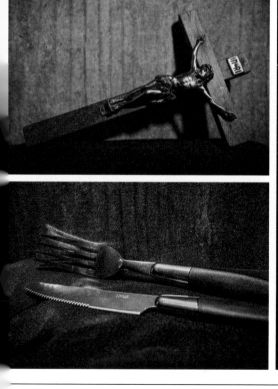

10.1

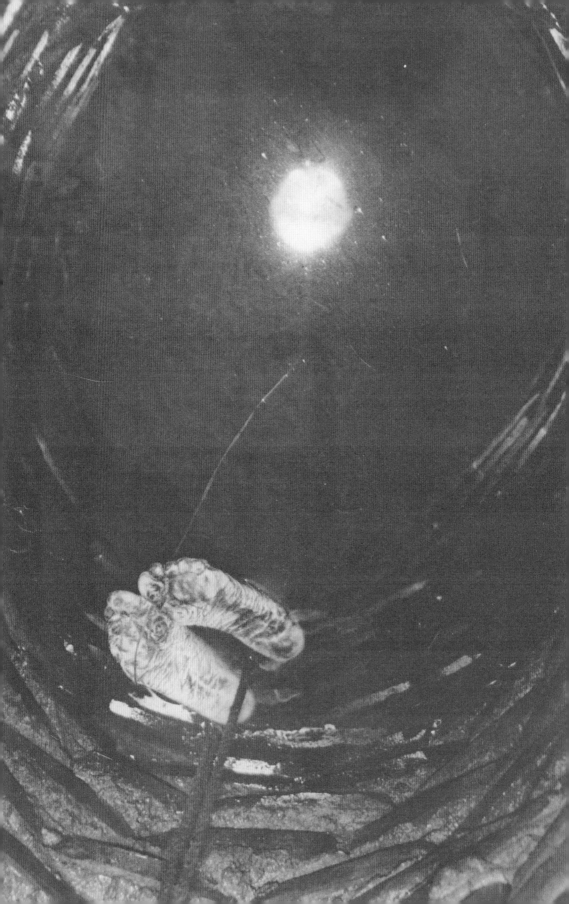

PORTRAITS OF THE DEAD

If a picture is worth a thousand words, then a picture of a dead body is surely worth ten thousand.

The earliest known photographs of criminals were taken within Belgian jails by prison officials in the 1840s. In England, between 1870 and 1872, over 43,000 crime photographs were taken and collected from across the country; however, due to the lack of consistency in the photographic technique, they were primarily stored to function as a rogues' gallery. It wasn't until 1890, when French policeman and biometrics researcher Alphonse Bertillon invented the "mug shot," that crime photography was taken seriously. More key developments swiftly followed in the early twentieth century, when the first unofficial forensic scientist, Edmond Locard, nicknamed the Sherlock Holmes of France, touted the importance of documenting a crime scene.

People collect crime scene photography as a way to get close to horrific events, albeit from a safe distance. It provides a two-dimensional experience of something they hope never to witness in person, and preserves moments in history that most people would like to forget. Geoff's collection contains original photo-graphs, from little-known and long-forgotten crimes to images of victims in high-profile murder cases. Regardless of the prominence of the case, all evoke visceral reactions, giving literal snapshots of people both living and dead in what is undoubtedly their darkest hour. They were photographed not to be exploited but to document a specific—albeit very macabre—moment in history.

When asked if he is seeking a "holy grail," Geoff enthusiastically refers to owning an album of crime images created by Bertillon. Referenced in *The Hound of the Baskervilles*, where Sherlock Holmes's clients refer to Holmes as the "second highest expert in Europe" after Bertillon, Alphonse is credited with many early advances in criminal science. "There's just something about French crime scenes that hit all the marks for me," says Geoff.

His collecting is not limited to the macabre, although most of it revolves around photography, with a concentration on mob-related crime scenes. Always on the lookout for the next "big hit," Geoff is actively searching for an original image of Joe "The Boss" Masseria holding the ace of spades after being whacked by his lieutenant, Charles "Lucky" Luciano.

The collection of Geoff

"You wanna see something wild?" These are the words that launched Geoff into the world of true crime collecting. "It was about nine years ago that an ephemera dealer I knew said that to me. Of course, I said 'Yes,' and he showed me eight police photos of a dead man who was severely burned from an arson fire. I was hooked."

Sometimes a prized piece has more to do with finding an emotional connection than the high-profile nature of the crime. Geoff says his "Information Wanted" poster from about 1957, for an unsolved case known as the Boy in the Box mystery, is an example of such an item: "It evolved into a local ghost story, and as kids, my friends and I would hang out in the woods where he was found."

True crime collecting undoubtedly leads to finding oneself in some unique situations, Geoff agrees. Though his most bizarre encounter had nothing directly to do with true crime collecting ... or, maybe it did? Geoff was at a flea market when an old-timer selling junk asked if Geoff was interested in a human skull. "I was intrigued, and at first glance, it appeared as normal a find as any medical skull. That was until I lifted it out of the cardboard box ... dirt cascaded out of it as if it was dug up just hours before the market. I did not buy it."

Photos by Dan Howell

1.1

1. Bundy Mug Shot

On August 16, 1975, Ted Bundy was arrested in Granger, Utah, after a pursuit where he attempted to evade a police officer. The Utah Highway Patrol incident report gives details: "He produced his driver's license, which identified him to be Theodore Robert Bundy ... I looked in the front, and there was no seat on the passenger side ... On the floor were some tools such as a jimmy bar ... they came up with a few other items of interest that a person coming from a movie normally would not carry, such as an ice pick, a pair of handcuffs, silk stockings with holes cut in for the eyes and nose." Bundy was arrested but, despite the situation, released on his own recognizance. He later stated that searchers missed a hidden collection of photographs of his victims, which he destroyed after being released.

1.1 **Bundy's police mug shot following his arrest in Utah on August 16, 1975, for evading a police officer.**

Portraits of the Dead

2. Sacrificial Murder

According to a front-page story in the February 9, 1933, edition of Kentucky's *Courier-Journal*, a series of odd events led up to the murder of Lucinda Mills. Before the incident, the Mills family were engaging in prayer, fasting, speaking in tongues, and turning sticks into snakes. As the fever of the ritual escalated, Mrs. Mills volunteered to be used as a human sacrifice, as an example of power over death in the name of God. John Mills began choking his mother to death as the remaining family members prayed, sang, and danced around the bed.

At some point in the murder, John Mills used a chain to continue strangling his mother and was intending to drag the body to a makeshift altar to burn the body when the police pushed their way into the cabin. John Mills was arrested along with seven other family members. They all pointed the accusing finger toward John, and he was ultimately sentenced to life in prison.

2.1 John Mills being led out of a community building by local authorities for the press to photograph the murderer.

2.2 A detective holding the chains that Mills used in the murder of his mother.

'The Mills family were engaging in prayer, fasting, speaking in tongues, and turning sticks into snakes.'

3. The Parsons Family

In 1906 an argument over money between 20-year-old Jodie Hamilton and Carney Parsons resulted in Hamilton killing the Parsons family in a brutal fashion, though the details of the crime vary. Hamilton shot Carney Parsons with a shotgun he was carrying, but the shot failed to kill him. Carney and his wife Minnie tried unsuccessfully to wrestle the weapon away before Hamilton struck Parsons a finishing blow to the head with the barrel of the gun. He then beat Mrs. Parsons to death and slit the throats of the couple's two older boys, aged six and three. Apparently, they did not die immediately, so he finished them off by crushing their skulls with the gun barrel. Finally, he battered the skull of their one-year-old brother to keep the infant's cries from attracting attention.

Hamilton was quickly apprehended and sentenced to be hanged. On Friday, December 21, 1906, at 11.02 a.m., 14 days after his 21st birthday, the trap was sprung. However, the knot at the end of the rope came loose and the noose slipped from Hamilton's neck. The officers picked Hamilton up from the ground below and carried him back up the 13 steps to the gallows. He was again placed on the re-set trap, and with Hamilton pleading "Don't draw it so tight—it is choking me," Sheriff Wood put the noose around his neck. At 11.04, the trap was sprung for a second time. The knot held, and Jodie Hamilton's soul plunged into eternity, accompanied by the cheers of an angry crowd.

3.1 **This haunting image is part memorial photograph, part evidence of Hamilton's horrible crime.**

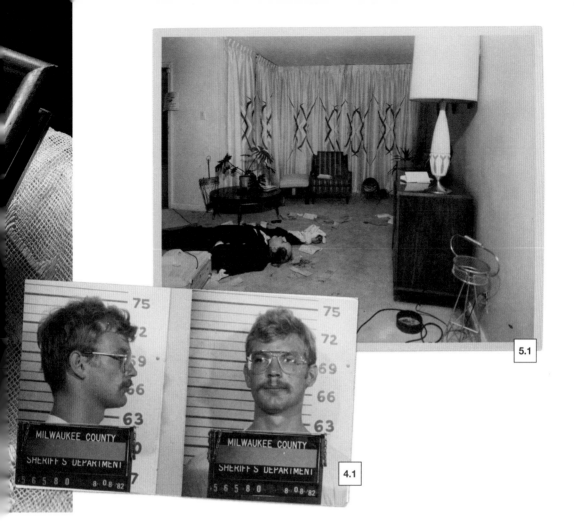

5.1

4.1

4. Indecent Exposure

In August 1982, when Jeffrey Dahmer was picked up and booked for indecent exposure, he already had one killing and numerous rapes under his belt. However, the courts were unaware of the murder, while the rapes were perpetrated against gay men, so apparently there wasn't any reason to prosecute him. He was given no jail time, just probation.

4.1 **Dahmer's police mug shot, taken on his arrest for indecent exposure in 1982.**

5. The Bookkeeper

5.1 This photo dates from the 1960s, a decade when crime was on the rise in America. It clearly depicts a crime scene in which a violent struggle had taken place before the murder.

The furniture has been tipped over, a television set is on the floor, and checks are strewn about. A closer look reveals that the victim's dentures have been knocked out and he took a bullet to the chest.

6. Self Portrait

6.1 A crime scene photographer from around the 1950s is himself captured in the mirror at a murder scene, where there has been a violent confrontation and shooting. [Over the page.]

6.1

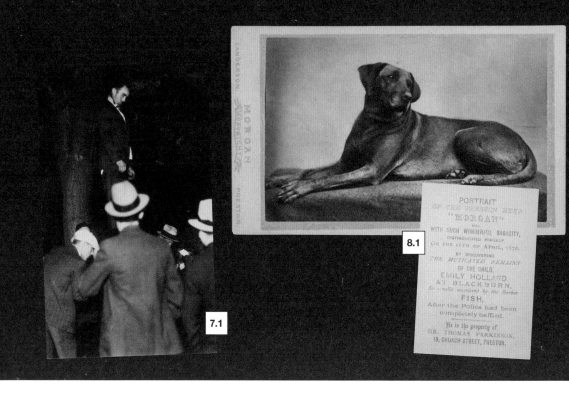

7.1

8.1

PORTRAIT
OF THE ...... HERO
"MORGAN"
WITH SUCH WONDERFUL SAGACITY,
DISTINGUISHED HIMSELF
ON THE 16TH OF APRIL, 1876,
BY DISCOVERING
THE MUTILATED REMAINS
OF THE CHILD,
EMILY HOLLAND
AT BLACKBURN,
So cruelly murdered by the Barber
FISH,
After the Police had been
completely baffled.

He is the property of
MR. THOMAS PARKINSON,
19, CHURCH STREET, PRESTON.

7. Lynch Mob Justice

On November 9, 1933, Thomas Harold
Thurmond and John M. Holmes kidnapped
22-year-old Brooke Hart, the eldest son of
Alexander Hart, owner of a popular department
store in San Jose, California. The pair asked for
a $40,000 ransom payment but, before waiting
to see if this would be paid, they bound Brooke's
hands and feet and dumped him into the San
Francisco Bay.

After being tracked down via a massive man-
hunt, followed by six hours of police interrogation,
Thurmond confessed and named his accomplice,
Holmes, in Brooke's kidnapping and murder. Just
two weeks later, on the evening of November 26,
a lynch mob smashed their way into the Santa
Clara County Jail and dragged Thurmond and
Holmes to St. James Park. There, with over 3,000
onlookers, the crowd chanted "string them up."

The San Jose Sheriff William Emig contacted
Governor James "Sunny Jim" Rolph, asking that
the National Guard be deployed to protect the
prisoners. The Governor refused.

7.1 This photo was taken before the lynch
mob yanked Thurmond's pants off.
Almost anyone who was lynched back then
was stripped naked first.

8. First Detection Dog

On March 28, 1876, seven-year-old Emily Agnes
Holland went missing from Blackburn, a town
in the north of England, after telling friends at
her school that she had met a nice man and was
going to run some errands for him. Two days
later, a child's naked torso was found in a field,
wrapped in blood-stained newspaper; the head,
arms, and legs were not at the location. That
afternoon the child's legs were found stuffed in
a drain not far away, also wrapped in newspaper.

On April 16 a dog by the name of Morgan was
taken to the home of suspect William Fish, where
he began to bark in front of the bedroom fire-
place. Upon inspection, the officers discovered
a human skull, hands, and forearms wrapped
in more blood-stained newspaper. Initially Fish
denied any involvement in the murder but later
confessed. He was hanged at Kirkdale jail in
Liverpool on August 14, 1876.

8.1 The case of William Fish was the first
recorded official use of dogs by police
to capture a murderer. The back of the photo
declares that Morgan distinguished himself
by discovering the child's remains "after the
police had been completely baffled."

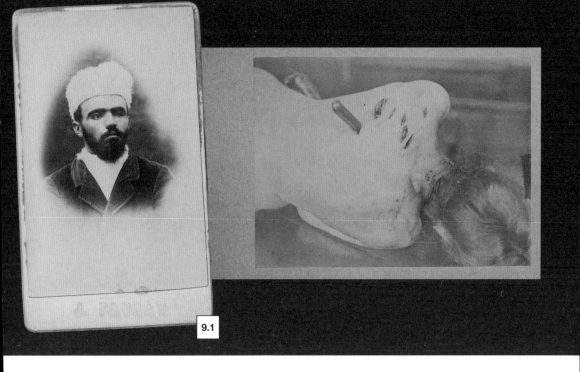

9.1

9. The French Ripper

Born in 1869, Joseph Vacher became infamously known as the French Ripper. Between 1894 and 1897, he is alleged to have murdered and mutilated at least 11 people: one woman, five teenage girls, and five teenage boys. Many of his victims were shepherds watching over their flocks in isolated locations. Vacher murdered his victims by stabbing them repeatedly, and often then disemboweled, raped, and sodomized them, the sexual activity at times happening post mortem.

In 1897 Vacher was caught attempting to rape a woman in a field in the Ardèche, and arrested. Despite trying to plead insanity, he was found guilty and sentenced to death on October 28, 1898. Two months later, on New Year's Eve 1898, Vacher was executed by the guillotine. He refused to walk to the scaffold and had to be dragged there by the executioner and the executioner's assistant.

9.1 An early nineteenth-century souvenir portrait card of Joseph Vacher, along with a grisly crime scene photo of one of Vacher's victims.

10. Death Car

Gangster Anthony Carfano, a capo in the Luciano crime family, was enjoying a meal at the New York restaurant Marino's when he was called away to take a mysterious emergency phone call. When he returned, he told his party that he must leave, stating "urgent business." Also leaving with him was the beautiful Janice Drake (former Miss New Jersey, 1944, and wife of the comedian Allan Drake), who he had offered to drive home.

Carfano was planning to drop Drake off at her apartment before heading to the airport to get a flight back to the safety of Miami. Unfortunately, in their haste to hit the road, the pair neglected to check the back seat of Carfano's Cadillac. At 10.15 p.m. the police were notified that a car was idling with its two front wheels up on the curb of 94th Street. Inside they discovered the dead bodies of Carfano and Drake. Carfano was slumped on the lap of Drake who, though dead, still looked ravishing. The double murder was a classic mob-style hit, both killed by bullets to the back of the head. No one was ever arrested.

10.1 Crime scene photo from the double murder of Anthony Carfano and Janice Drake in 1959. [Over the page.]

10.1

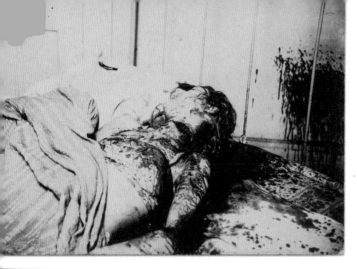

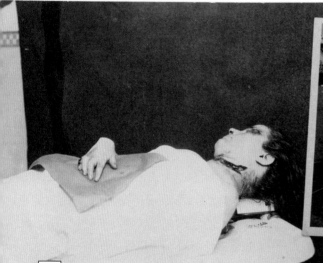

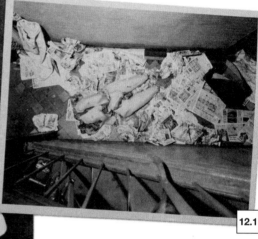

11. Respect for the Dead

The blood on the wall, the blood-soaked bedding, the hair caked with dried blood, and, of course, the gaping neck wound make it clear that the female victim in this photo died from her jugular vein being slashed. In the second photo, the coroner has cleaned the body, including washing the victim's hair. The neck wound is still clearly visible, and the victim's hand is also on display, possibly to show a defensive wound.

12. The Torso Killer

In November 1964, New York City police had the unpleasant task of identifying three dismembered bodies found in various parts of the city. The police stated they were "not ruling out that a maniac might have slain all three."

It wasn't until the apprehension of "the Torso Killer" Richard Cottingham in 1980 that law enforcement began to link a series of murders characterized by dismemberment to him. Although he has not admitted to the three cases in 1964, many believe he is the culprit.

Even from the distance of the first photo, it is fairly clear that what lies ahead is not pleasant. On closer inspection those fears are confirmed.

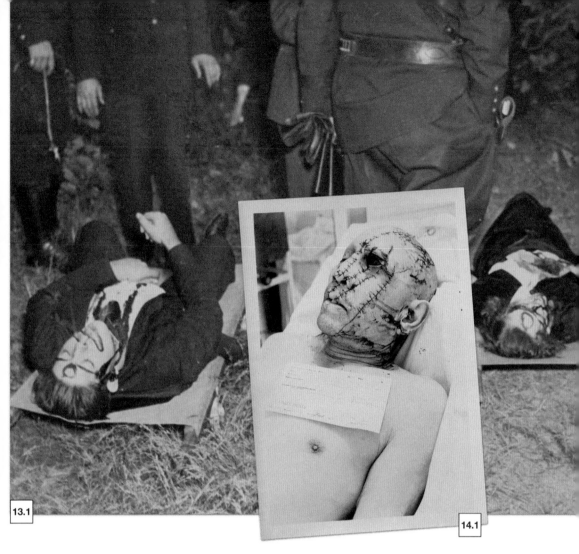

13.1

14.1

13. The Red Circle Slayer

It was a cool October morning in 1937 when a grisly and tragic discovery was made in a suburb of New York City. The bodies of two young lovers, Lewis Weiss, 20, and Frances Hajek, 19, were found brutally murdered. Weiss was slumped over in the front seat of his car, dead from two bullets to the head. Hajek suffered a more horrific end, with two bullets to the temple and seven stab wounds to her chest from an ice pick. Before leaving the scene, the killer further defiled his victims by drawing a blood-red circle on each of their foreheads with Hajek's lipstick. Although police followed up countless leads, the case went unsolved.

13.1 Crime scene photograph from the unsolved murders of Lewis Weiss and Frances Hajek.

14. Meat Cleaver

14.1 This murder victim is about to undergo an autopsy, but his face was first pieced back together by the coroner after he was attacked with a meat cleaver — not by a crazed serial killer, as one might expect, but a brutal act perpetrated by his own wife. We can only wonder what events might have prompted such a violent crime.

FROM GEIN TO GACY

Discussions of the ethical issues surrounding serial killer art are ongoing, but none is as hotly debated as that by John Wayne Gacy. When Gacy was first isolated on death row, he began to paint, primarily portraits of his alter egos, the clowns Pogo and Patches. When asked by a reporter why he started painting, Gacy replied, "to bring joy to people's lives."

Psychiatrists, psychoanalysts, and art therapists, among countless other experts, have theorized about the psychosexual meaning behind the content of Gacy's work. There is speculation as to why someone who was a sexual deviant always painted himself from the waist up. Was he subconsciously cutting off his genitalia? Did he paint himself in a three-quarter view with his left hand raised to echo the way Christ is depicted in traditional religious paintings? Although never proven, there are also rumors that Gacy ran his artistic endeavors in an Andy Warhol-type production line by teaching other inmates how to paint Pogo in the Gacy style so he could fulfill the number of requests he was receiving from collectors of crime art.

Until he saw a documentary on serial killers and their artistic endeavors behind bars, collector Jerry G. had no idea you could own a Gacy Pogo painting. Since his original Pogo purchase, Jerry has curated an impressive Gacy art collection, including "Blood Skull," "Dahmer Skull," "Single Skull," "Double Skull," "Skull Clown," "Indian Skull," and "Death Wish." He also has a rare "Goodbye Pogo the Clown."

Jerry has his own theory on Gacy and why he did what he did. "For me, Gacy is one of those figures that epitomizes evil. When people tell me Gacy was crazy, I tell them, no, he wasn't crazy. He was just evil. He knew exactly what he was doing and functioned in normal society very well. Which only made it easier for him to embrace his evil side, torturing and killing at least 30 people."

Jerry G.

The collection of Jerry G.

Jerry's collection touches upon many periods and historical events, with a sweet spot for mob-related pieces and serial killer items. Two pieces that he finds extraordinary fall into very different categories. The first is a 1692 Salem witch trial document signed by Samuel Sewall. The other is an original Edward Gein-signed fingerprint chart. Gein is one of those figures who transcends true crime fans and was the inspiration for many iconic Hollywood "monsters," including Leatherface, Buffalo Bill, and Norman Bates.

Another historical villain that makes their way back into pop culture every couple of decades, catching the interest of a new generation, is Lizzie Borden. Jerry is actively seeking something that includes her signature. "My response to people who are offended by true crime collecting is simple. I am not a proponent of what's now become known as 'cancel culture,' which includes people trying to erase or ignore that there were, still are, and unfortunately will continue to be many people who will make a mark on society. In this case, a dark mark. And that dark mark still has historical significance."

Photos by Dan Howell

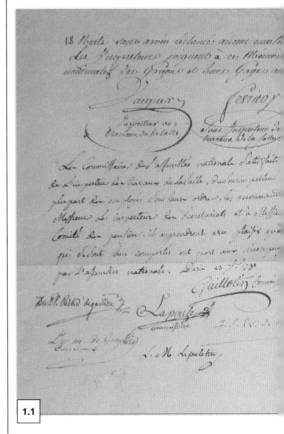

1.1

1. Painless and Humane

Throughout the eighteenth and nineteenth centuries, a multitude of crimes were punishable by death. Methods of execution included burning at the stake, the breaking wheel, death by boiling, and dismemberment, but the most likely were beheading with an ax or hanging from the gallows. Although these last two may *seem* more humane, they weren't. Cutting off a head with an ax or a sword did not always cause immediate death, while the technique of hanging had not been perfected and most victims slowly suffocated to death.

French physician and politician Joseph Guillotin was opposed to the death penalty. However, he realized that trying to end executions was futile and decided to lobby to at least make them more humane. On October 10, 1789, a new device to carry out the death penalty in France in a "painless and humane manner" was used on a highwayman named Nicolas Jacques Pelletier. Guillotin was not in fact the guillotine's inventor,

2.1

3.1

although his name has become an eponym for it. One Tobias Schmidt was the actual inventor of the prototype.

1.1 An extremely rare French Revolution era-dated document signed by Guillotin.

2. Televised Suicide

Budd Dwyer was a Pennsylvania State Senator facing bribery charges. On January 23, 1987, Dwyer held a press conference at which he produced a manila envelope and pulled out a .357 Magnum revolver. It quickly became apparent to the crowd what Dwyer's intentions were. There were cries for him to stop, and it appeared as though someone was approaching him to prevent him from killing himself, but Dwyer shoved the nose of the gun up into his mouth and pulled the trigger. The cameraman never took his lens off Dwyer and, in fact, zoomed in as he lay there dead and bleeding profusely.

2.1 Assorted original Dwyer campaign material for several different offices he held over his political career.

3. Deranged Fan

On July 1, 1989, after three years of stalking Rebecca Schaeffer, the female star of the TV show *My Sister Sam*, Robert Bardo shot and killed Schaeffer. He was arrested the next day and eventually sentenced to life in prison without the possibility of parole. On July 27, 2007, Bardo was stabbed 11 times on his way to breakfast in the maximum-security unit at Mule Creek State Prison. He survived the attack and continues to serve his life sentence at Avenal State Prison in California.

3.1 A Bardo drawing of Schaeffer lies beside an autographed headshot that Bardo used as a reference.

4. Ed Gein's Fingerprints

Although Edward Gein, "the Plainfield Ghoul," has only been "credited" with two confirmed murders, he holds a place of distinction among the list of serial killers. His infamy comes via his grave robbery, which, on his capture and the subsequent search of his Plainfield, Wisconsin, property, revealed a house of horrors. Along with a murdered woman's decapitated body in a shed, hung upside down by ropes at her wrists, the authorities discovered: four noses; whole human bones; nine masks of human skin; bowls made from human skulls; ten female heads; human skin covering several chair seats; Mary Hogan's head in a paper bag; Bernice Worden's head in a burlap sack; nine vulvas in a shoebox; skulls on his bedposts; organs in the refrigerator; a pair of lips on a drawstring for a window shade; a belt made from human female nipples; and a lampshade made from the skin from a human face.

Gein was arrested on November 17, 1957, and after three trials, was ultimately found legally insane, spending the rest of his life in a psychiatric facility until he died in 1984.

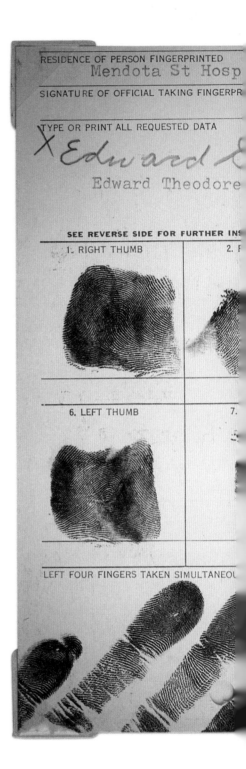

4.1 **Original Edward Gein-signed fingerprint chart, and a tabloid newspaper taking advantage of the horrible crimes.**

'The authorities discovered: four noses; whole human bones; nine masks of human skin; bowls made from human skulls; ten female heads; human skin covering several chair seats ...'

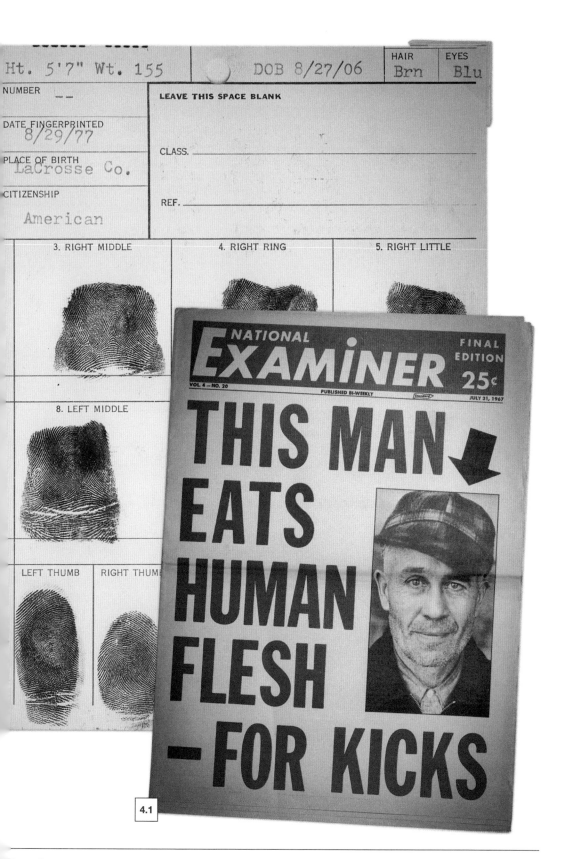

5. Peoples Temple Death Cult

Jim Jones was a preacher and civil rights activist who went on to become the cult leader of the Peoples Temple, with a following of over a thousand. Things were "all good" until November 15, 1978, when Congressman Leo Ryan flew to Jonestown, Guyana, to investigate claims of human rights abuses. Jones believed that Ryan was about to return home with information that would be detrimental to his reputation. While boarding the plane with some former cult members, Congressman Ryan was shot and killed along with four others. Later that day, Jones ordered a mass suicide by drinking grape Flavor Aid laced with cyanide. As a result, 918 people died an agonizing death.

5.1 Jones's senior high-school yearbook, church services sheet, propaganda booklet, and a press photo of Jones's body.

6. Bundy's Yearbook

One of the things that allowed Ted Bundy to carry out his crimes on unsuspecting women was his clean-cut appearance. He would eventually confess to the killing of 30 women and girls, and was executed by electrocution in Florida in 1989.

6.1 Ted Bundy's high-school yearbook, in which a fresh-faced Bundy poses for his senior photo.

7. Columbine Killers

On the morning of April 20, 1999, students Eric Harris and Dylan Klebold entered Columbine High School in Columbine, Colorado, and fired a total of 188 rounds of ammunition, killing 12 students and one teacher. Harris and Klebold committed suicide on-site.

7.1 The 2002 commencement ceremony booklet, which includes students from the last year anyone involved with that tragic day graduated, plus a memorial sheet for the students and teachers who died. The 1999 Revelations Yearbook for Columbine High contains photos of Harris and Klebold; these were never removed.

5.1

Ted Bundy

6.1

'The 1999 Revelations Yearbook for Columbine High contains photos of Harris and Klebold; these were never removed.'

7.1

8.1

8.2

8. The Killer Clown

In December 1978, the infamous John Wayne Gacy was convicted of torturing and murdering 33 young men. He spent 16 years in a maximum-security prison and became a very prolific (albeit not very accomplished) artist. Gacy's paintings became highly sought after, with collectors ranging from crime enthusiasts to Hollywood celebrities.

8.1 This is one of only a few known press photos of John Wayne Gacy dressed as his alter ego Pogo the Clown.

8.2 According to Gacy, there were "four Johns." The first three—John the contractor, John the clown, and John the politician—are pictured here. The fourth "John" went by the name of Jack Hanley, and he was the killer. He is apparently not depicted in this self-portrait ... or is he?

8.3 A rare "Goodbye Pogo the Clown" painting, with the left hand raised. Very few of these were painted before Gacy's execution (one can also be seen on page 154 in the collection of Stephen Giannangelo). Although Pogo paintings are fairly common, this is a rare early Pogo and an even rarer Patches. The card in the foreground is a pop-up made by Larry Bittaker, one of the despicable Tool Box Killers, who, along with Roy Norris, kidnapped, raped, tortured, and killed five teenage girls in southern California over a five-month period in 1979. On page 96 you can see a one-of-a-kind "Pogo the Clown" bust created by Canadian artist Steve Bellamy of the studio The Devil's Latex.

8.4 A series of original Gacy skull-themed paintings. Left to right: "Double Skull," "Skull Clown," "Indian Skull."

by Henry Lee Lucas

9.1

10.1

Ottis Toole

c. m.

Ottis Elwood Toole
4-30-93

Ottis Toole

9. Deviant Art

Henry Lee Lucas was convicted of 11 murders, but like his partner in crime, Ottis Toole (below), he claims the number of his victims to be in the hundreds. The similarities between their deviant characters are evident in their painting styles.

9.1 These paintings are entitled "Decaying Clown" and "Dracula" (the clown resembling Ottis Toole).

10. Deadly Duo

Later called "the Jacksonville Cannibal," drifter Ottis Toole had a few murders under his belt before he met fellow psychopath Henry Lee Lucas in 1976. However, the pairing upped Toole's "game," and from 1976 through 1983, he claims to have raped and killed anywhere from six to 65 people, mostly young boys, including Adam Walsh, son of *America's Most Wanted* creator John Walsh.

10.1 These drawings give a peek into the mind of a man who would want to lay claim to such a disturbing declaration. Between them sits a signed in-prison Polaroid of Toole.

11. Pins and Needles

The Gray Man, the Werewolf of Wysteria, the Brooklyn Vampire, the Moon Maniac, and the Boogey Man were all monikers the tabloids of the 1930s draped upon a monster whose real name was Hamilton Howard "Albert" Fish.

In reality, Fish was a deranged individual: a serial killer, child rapist, and cannibal, who claimed to have killed as many as 100 victims (primarily children). A true sadomasochist, Fish said he enjoyed inflicting pain—especially on young boys—and being in pain himself. He told a prison psychiatrist that he had been sticking needles into his body for years, mainly in the area between his rectum and scrotum: "He told of doing it to other people too, especially children," reported the psychiatrist. The doctor thought Fish was lying and had him X-rayed. The film revealed over 25 needles buried into his perineum.

11.1 On December 13, 1934, Fish was arrested and executed via electrocution at Ossining Correctional Facility (Sing Sing) on January 16, 1936. This very rare court document includes Fish's signature.

12. Salem Witch Trials

The infamous Salem witchcraft trials took place in Massachusetts in 1692. A group of young girls, swept up in a wave of hysteria, claimed to be possessed and accused many of their neighbors of witchcraft, ultimately causing 19 innocent men and women to be hanged as witches.

12.1 New England Puritan Samuel Sewall served as chief justice of the Massachusetts Superior Court of Judicature for many years, and took part in the decision-making that condemned the "witches." However, Sewall regretted his involvement and even called for a public day of prayer, fasting, and reparations. He also believed that God punished him for his involvement. In the five years following the trials, two of his daughters died, along with his wife's mother. His wife also gave birth to a stillborn child. Shown here is a document signed by Samuel Sewall and dated 1692.

12.2 Jonathan Corwin was one of the first judges to be called on to make early inquiries into the reports of witchcraft. His home, known as the Witch House of Salem, is still standing and is the only remaining structure with direct ties to the Salem witch trials. This Corwin-signed document is dated from the early 1700s.

12.3 Thomas Danforth was a magistrate and leading figure in the Massachusetts colony at the Salem witch trials. Danforth was reported to be a domineering governor, but the truth is he was critical of the trials and was instrumental in bringing them to an end.

12.4 John Hathorne was a judge at the Salem witch trials and a vocal magistrate who used a publication to promote the trials. There is no record of Hathorne having been repentant for participating in the trials. This document is signed John Hathorne Just Ps (Justice of the Peace).

12.1

12.2

12.3

12.4

MENARD TRANS. REC'D.
81114

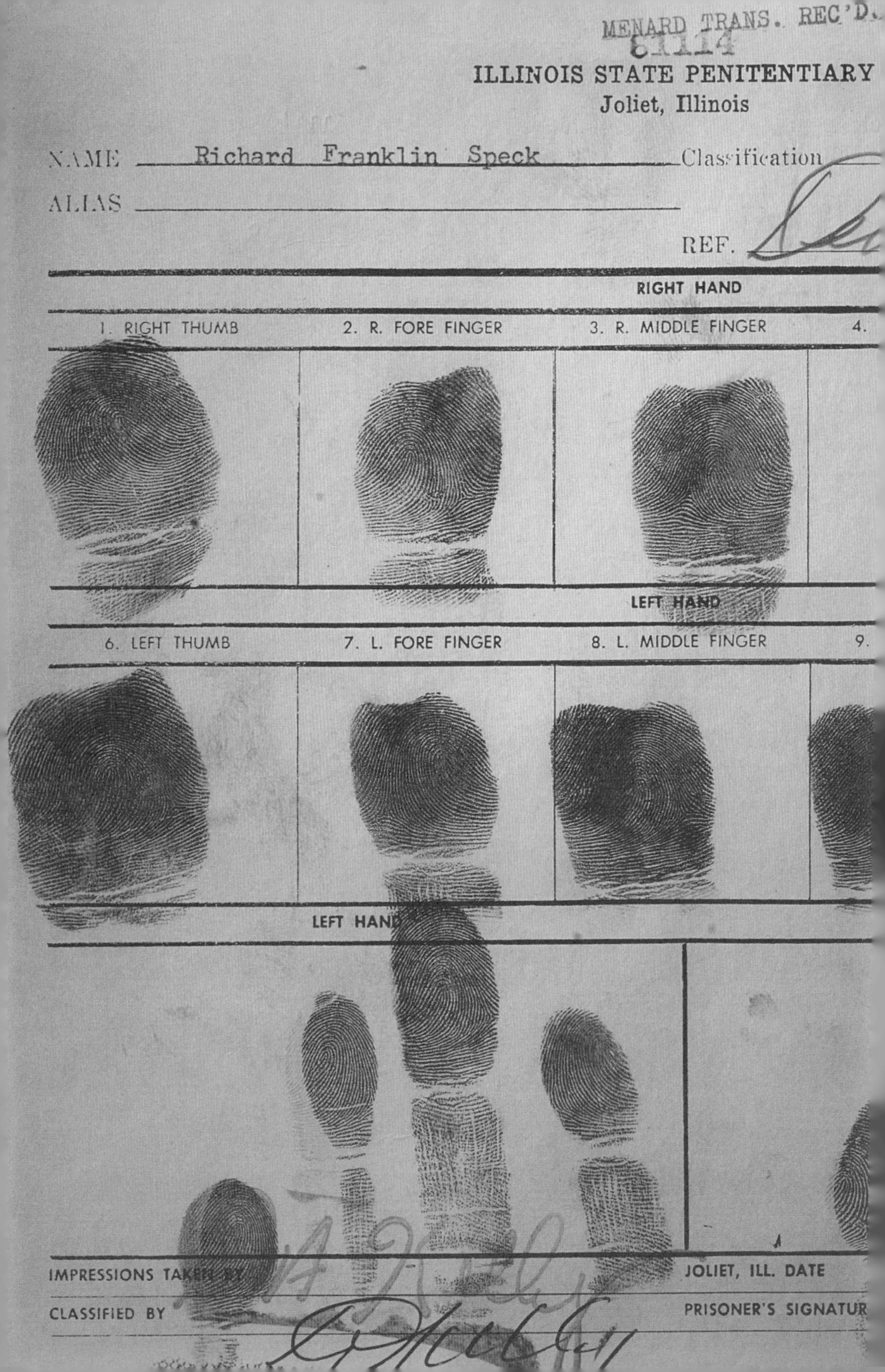

ILLINOIS STATE PENITENTIARY
Joliet, Illinois

NAME Richard Franklin Speck Classification

ALIAS

REF.

RIGHT HAND

1. RIGHT THUMB 2. R. FORE FINGER 3. R. MIDDLE FINGER 4.

LEFT HAND

6. LEFT THUMB 7. L. FORE FINGER 8. L. MIDDLE FINGER 9.

LEFT HAND

IMPRESSIONS TAKEN BY

JOLIET, ILL. DATE

CLASSIFIED BY

PRISONER'S SIGNATUR

CRIME
&
PUNISHMENT

Up to the early twentieth century, public executions were intended as a spectacle to reinforce the public's faith that law and order remained in place, and as a warning to any potential offenders that crime doesn't pay. (Ironically, many of those who gathered to witness these executions found themselves pickpocketed by bands of thieves who sifted their way through the mob.) By the nineteenth century, these public executions had become an unofficial source of entertainment, with trinkets, postcards, and even bits of the hangman's rope being sold as souvenirs. On occasion, the crowd was sympathetic to the criminal being hanged and would threaten the guards and rush the gallows, causing dozens of spectators to be crushed or suffocated to death.

Certain items in Nathan's collection—such as pieces made from the skin of inmates and jars of human fat harvested from executed prisoners—make you question what kind of people were running the penal system 100 years ago. Indeed, many of the "fortunate" souls who found themselves incarcerated instead of executed may soon have wished for the latter fate

since, throughout the centuries, life behind bars has always been a living hell.

Other historical treasures relating to the penal system in Nathan's collection include a "Table of Drops" document, an early indicator of prison reform, with its attempt to develop a more humane method of hanging a man. His most prized possession is the logbook and measuring tape that belonged to English hangman Henry Pierrepoint. The logbook records the names, heights, and weights of all the people Pierrepoint hanged, with details of their crimes. It is a fascinating handwritten record from a man who was personally responsible for snuffing out the lives of some of England's worst criminals at the end of a rope. "It is a museum-worthy piece, and I'm amazed that I own it."

"Over the years, my collection has grown based on the philosophy: If an item catches my attention, or I think it is important, I'll buy it. I don't care what it is. Authenticity is essential. Because, as far as I'm concerned, I'm preserving history. Most historical items don't need protection, but some people are actively trying to destroy this stuff."

The collection of Nathan

Nathan was in high school and already a serious autograph collector when people in that scene began acquiring prisoner autographs. He was into true crime, and it seemed like a natural extension of his existing hobby. Nathan's attention was captured by a documentary on the serial killer Hadden Clark, and he felt compelled to write to him. Not only did Clark respond, but he began sending letters, drawings, and weird items like fingernail clippings and jewelry made of dental picks.

Since that first contact, Nathan has curated a very serious true crime and punishment collection. "Like it or not, crime is an essential part of history. I purchased a Dahmer item once solely to stop the owner from burning it. I've sold some important documents, photographs, and diaries from my collection to an Ivy League University for their special collections and archives department. Those items are now going to be accessed by authors, researchers, and historians for generations to come."

Like most collectors, there is that one piece that has so far eluded him. In Nathan's case, it's an electric chair: a real one. Although many people claim to own one of these, he knows of only one in private hands that he is convinced is the genuine article.

Photos by Dan Howell

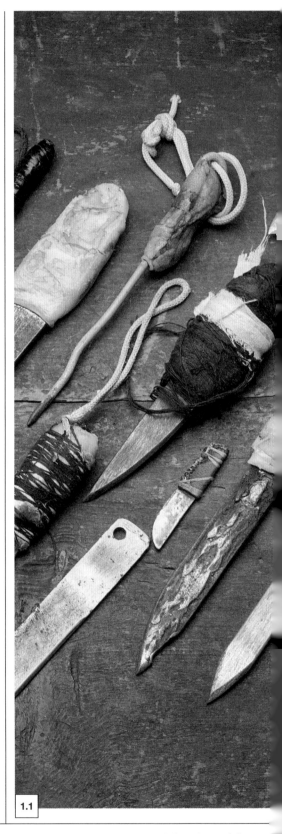

1.1

1. Shivs

Hundreds of prisoners are killed by other inmates every year. Many of these fatalities come with the aid of prison-made weapons. Prisoners are incredibly resourceful and have made makeshift knives, known as shanks or shivs, out of many innocuous items, including toothbrushes, Styrofoam cups, candy and cigarette filters (melted and molded into a point and a sharp edge), disposable razors, metal from ventilators, batteries, and even paper hardened with toothpaste and then sharpened.

1.1 An array of prison-made weapons. It's impossible to know how many of these may have been used to kill or maim fellow inmates or indeed prison guards.

2. Macabre Memento

2.1 A Missouri prison guard, who was evidently more demented than most of the prisoners he was paid to watch over, apparently made this wallet from the skin of a deceased inmate around the 1930s.

2.1

3. Black Charley

In September 1903, Maryland citizen Charles Jones was arrested and eventually convicted of murder. He was only 12 years old. At that young age, he already had a criminal nickname: "Black Charley."

3.1 This rare early twentieth century mug shot/booking card has Jones's height at only 4 foot 5½ inches, and his eye color is peculiarly described as "maroon."

4. The Measuring Man

In May 1961 Albert DeSalvo was arrested for Assault and Battery and Breaking and Entering. This was the fourth time he had been detained since 1956 and, although not initially arrested for it, he admitted during the 1961 arrest to being the "Measuring Man," whom the police had been hunting in connection with a series of sexual assaults. As the "Measuring Man," DeSalvo would knock on doors looking for young women to molest, introducing himself as a talent scout from the "Black and White Modeling Agency." As part of the "interview" DeSalvo would ask to take their measurements and proceed to fondle them while doing so.

DeSalvo would later confess to being the Boston Strangler, claiming 13 female victims. Although, at the time, DeSalvo's claims were disputed, 49 years later cold-case DNA testing incontrovertibly linked him to the crimes.

4.1 A Cambridge Police Department booking card from DeSalvo's arrest in 1961. It lists his father's name as "not known."

'As the "Measuring Man," Albert DeSalvo would knock on doors looking for young women to molest.'

3.1

SACHUSETTS DEPARTMENT OF PUBLIC SAFETY, BUREAU OF IDENTIFICATION
1010 Commonwealth Avenue, Boston 15, Massachusetts

Department or Institution .... Location

bert Henry De Salvo .... NAME TYPED OR PRINTED Albert Henry De Salvo

Florence St. Park Malden Mass.

MARRIED, SINGLE, WIDOW, WIDOWER, DIVORCED Married

Not Known .... COUNTRY OF BIRTH Not Known

Charlott Roberts .... COUNTRY OF BIRTH Not Known

Irngard Beck .... ADDRESS Same

DATE OF BIRTH 10/3/31 .... BIRTHPLACE Chelsea Massachusetts

WEIGHT 174 .... HAIR Brown .... EYES Hazel .... BUILD

te .... CITIZENSHIP Born .... OCCUPATION Pressman

CH AS MARKS, SCARS, TATTOOS, AMPUTATIONS, MOUSTACHE, BEARD, MISSING, FALSE OR IRREGULAR TEETH, BLINDNESS, EYE
OSTURE, ACCENTS, HABITS OR PECULIARITIES, ETC., WITH DATE OF ORIGIN IF KNOWN:

T Cambridge Police .... Date 5/5/61

3 4 Cts & Att. B&E. D/T 6(2yrs) conc. Fr 5/3/61 Less 5 Das

t 5/5/61

t, date,
rges)

name in full, professional,
through previous marriages

(If "Yes", give dates, p
& prison numbers as a

FBI No.

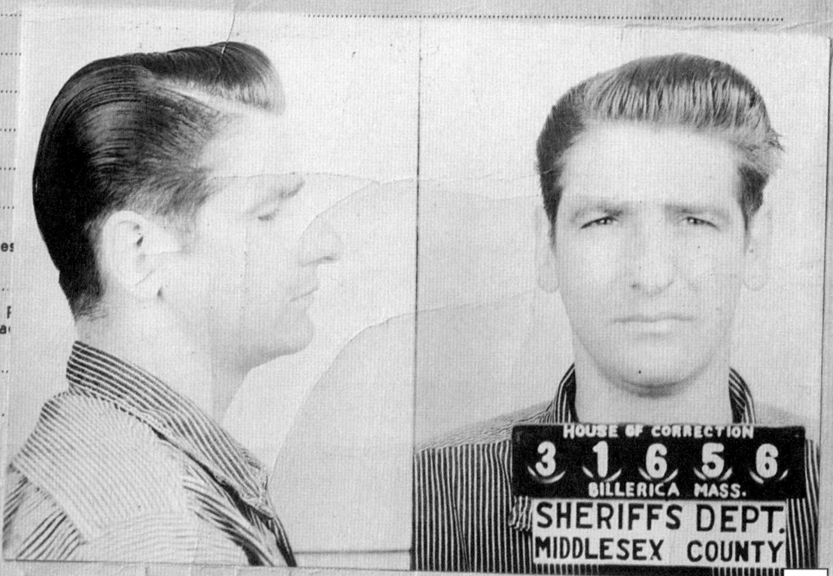

4.1

5.1

6.1

5. A Big Man of God

At a towering 6 foot 9 inches, Edmund Kemper was an imposing figure. Add in a high IQ of 145, a diagnosis of paranoid schizophrenia, and an apparent bloodlust, and you have one terrifying individual convicted of killing ten people (including his paternal grandparents).

5.1 | **A Bible owned by Kemper, still in its original box. Inside Kemper has written "this has been with me through a lot of good and bad times."**

6. Jesus Loves Aileen

In the weeks before her execution, Aileen Wuornos gave a series of interviews to English documentary filmmaker Nicholas Broomfield, in which she spoke about "being taken away to meet God and Jesus and the angels and whatever is beyond the beyond."

6.1 | **This was Aileen Wuornos's personal Bible. The cover is inscribed with the notation "Jesus Loves Aileen."**

7. Born-again Dahmer

Shortly after Jeffrey Dahmer's arrest on July 22, 1991, and a lengthy 60-hour interview in which he admitted to killing 16 of his 17 victims, Dahmer requested a copy of the Bible from Detective Murphy (one of the two detectives that took down Dahmer's 160-page confession). Dahmer was given the Bible and went on to become a born-again Christian. In 1994, Roy Ratcliff, a minister in the Church of Christ, baptized Dahmer in the prison whirlpool.

7.1 | **Dahmer's well-thumbed personal Bible, with notations and cell and inmate numbers written on the inside cover page.**

(handwritten, upper right)
Jeff Dahmer #227252
Columbia Corr. Inst. S.M.O.
Portage, WI 53901-0900

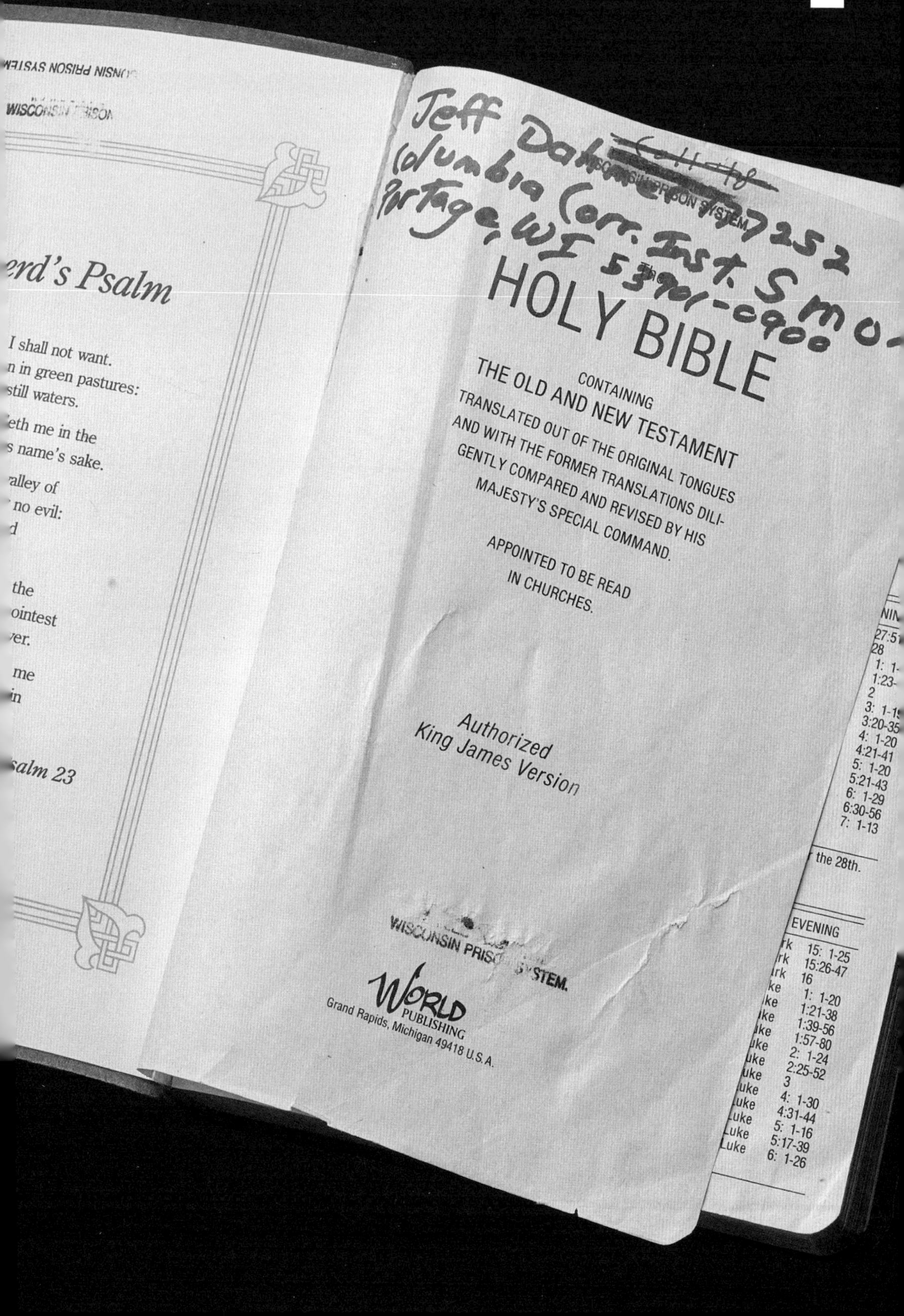

WISCONSIN PRISON SYSTEM

HOLY BIBLE

CONTAINING

THE OLD AND NEW TESTAMENT

TRANSLATED OUT OF THE ORIGINAL TONGUES
AND WITH THE FORMER TRANSLATIONS DILI-
GENTLY COMPARED AND REVISED BY HIS
MAJESTY'S SPECIAL COMMAND.

APPOINTED TO BE READ
IN CHURCHES.

Authorized
King James Version

WISCONSIN PRISON SYSTEM.

WORLD
PUBLISHING
Grand Rapids, Michigan 49418 U.S.A.

(left page, partially visible)

...erd's Psalm

...I shall not want.
...in green pastures:
...still waters.

...eth me in the
...s name's sake.

...alley of
...no evil:
...d

...the
...ointest
...er.

...me
...n

...salm 23

(right edge, partially visible column)

NIN
27:5
28
1: 1
1:23-
2
3: 1-1
3:20-35
4: 1-20
4:21-41
5: 1-20
5:21-43
6: 1-29
6:30-56
7: 1-13

the 28th.

EVENING

rk	15: 1-25
rk	15:26-47
rk	16
ke	1: 1-20
ke	1:21-38
ke	1:39-56
ke	1:57-80
uke	2: 1-24
uke	2:25-52
uke	3
uke	4: 1-30
Luke	4:31-44
Luke	5: 1-16
Luke	5:17-39
Luke	6: 1-26

Return to F.o.W.

EXECUTIONS.—Table of Drops (October, 1913).

The length of the drop may usually be calculated by dividing 1,000 foot-pounds by the weight of the culprit and his clothing in pounds, which will give the length of the drop in feet, but no drop should exceed 8 feet 6 inches. Thus a person weighing 150 pounds in his clothing will ordinarily require a drop of 1,000 divided by 150 = $6\frac{2}{3}$ feet, *i.e.*, 6 feet 8 inches. The following table is calculated on this basis up to the weight of 200 pounds:—

TABLE OF DROPS.

Weight of the Prisoner in his Clothes.	Length of the Drop.		Weight of the Prisoner in his Clothes.	Length of the Drop.		Weight of the Prisoner in his Clothes.	Length of the Drop.	
lbs.	ft.	ins.	lbs.	ft.	ins.	lbs.	ft.	ins.
118 and under	8	6	138 and under	7	3	167 and under	6	0
119 ,,	8	5	140 ,,	7	2	169 ,,	5	11
120 ,,	8	4	141 ,,	7	1	171 ,,	5	10
121 ,,	8	3	143 ,,	7	0	174 ,,	5	9
122 ,,	8	2	145 ,,	6	11	176 ,,	5	8
124 ,,	8	1	146 ,,	6	10	179 ,,	5	7
125 ,,	8	0	148 ,,	6	9	182 ,,	5	6
126 ,,	7	11	150 ,,	6	8	185 ,,	5	5
128 ,,	7	10	152 ,,	6	7	188 ,,	5	4
129 ,,	7	9	154 ,,	6	6	190 ,,	5	3
130 ,,	7	8	156 ,,	6	5	194 ,,	5	2
132 ,,	7	7	158 ,,	6	4	197 ,,	5	1
133 ,,	7	6	160 ,,	6	3	200 ,,	5	0
135 ,,	7	5	162 ,,	6	2			
136 ,,	7	4	164 ,,	6	1			

When for any special reason, such as a diseased condition of the neck of the culprit, the Governor and Medical Officer think that there should be a departure from this table, they may inform the executioner, and advise him as to the length of the drop which should be given in that particular case.

(C 48704) 100 4/43.

8.1

Mr. *J. L. Hartman*
Your presence is requested at White Sulphur Springs, Montana, on the morning of Friday, February Sixteenth, in the Year of Our Lord Nineteen Hundred Seventeen, to witness the execution of

HENRY HALL
HARRISON GIBSON
LESTER FAHLEY

R.S.V.P.

GEO. B. NAGUES
Sheriff of Meagher County, Montana.

9.1

8. Table of Drops

The Official Table of Drops was issued by the British Home Office in 1888 after a number of failed hangings, including those of John "Babbacombe" Lee, a convicted murderer who was hanged unsuccessfully three times and ultimately let free. The Table is used to calculate the appropriate length of rope for long-drop hangings and continued to be used in the United Kingdom until the country suspended capital punishment in 1965. The UK abolished the death penalty altogether in 1998, but the Table remains in use in former British colonies that have retained capital punishment by hanging, such as Singapore.

8.1 This Table of Drops document dates from August 1913.

9. Invitation to a Hanging

Harrison Gibson, Henry Hall, and Lester Fahley (aka King Faro) were hanged for murder in a triple hanging. The three convicts were from a group of seven railway workers who robbed a train. Gibson, Hall, and Fahley shot their victims after the robbery, which earned them the death penalty.

9.1 A 1917 invitation to witness the execution of Lester Fahley, a member of one of America's first Black gangs, with his photograph and a section of the rope that was used to hang him.

10. The Hangman's Log

Henry Pierrepoint was an early twentieth-century English hangman (and father of Albert Pierrepoint, England's "most prolific" hangman, having executed over 400 people). Henry's personal logbook includes a written log of every one of the 105 hangings that he performed.

10.1 The book is opened to the page of the famous double execution of two women in the "baby farming case," the only double hanging of women in modern times. The tape measure was used by Henry Pierrepoint in his nine-year tenure as executioner.

11.1

11. Babes in the Wood

On November 24, 1934, the bodies of Norma Sedgwick, 12, Dewilla Noakes, 10, and Cordelia Noakes, 8, were found under a blanket in the woods along a Pennsylvania road. The girls had been suffocated, presumably by Elmo Noakes, father of Dewilla and Cordelia, and Norma's stepfather. The next day, Elmo shot and killed his 18-year-old niece Winifred Pierce before killing himself with a .22 rifle. The media dubbed the chilling find the Babes in the Wood Murders.

11.1 An original photograph of the scene, which was printed widely in newspapers in the hope that someone could identify the victims, along with an advertising flyer for Eckels Soluble Masks that includes the image of the deceased children. Death masks of the children had been made before they were buried to aid in the identification process.

12. Alphabet Murders

Between 1971 and 1973, Rochester, New York, experienced a series of killings, dubbed the Alphabet Murders. All three victims were girls aged ten or eleven, whose surnames began with the same letter as their first names. Each one was sexually assaulted and murdered, and her body discarded in or near a town beginning with the same letter as the victim's name.

12.1 Poster offering a $10,000 reward "for information leading to the arrest and conviction of the killer of Wanda Walkowicz," the second girl to go missing. The Alphabet Murders remain unsolved.

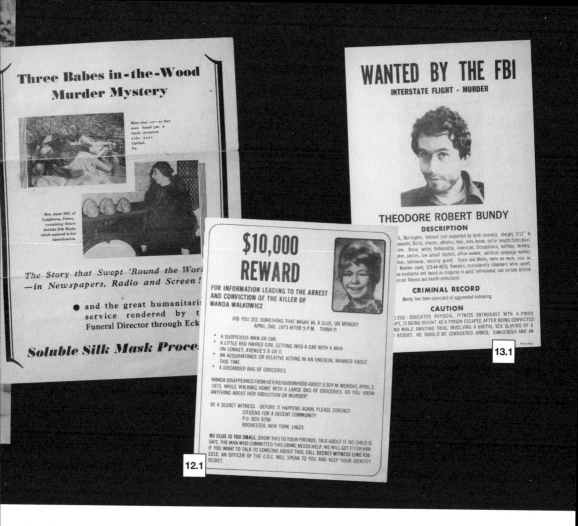

Three Babes in-the-Wood Murder Mystery

The Story that Swept 'Round the Worl —in Newspapers, Radio and Screen!

- and the great humanitari:
  service rendered by t
  Funeral Director through Eck

Soluble Silk Mask Proce

$10,000 REWARD

FOR INFORMATION LEADING TO THE ARREST
AND CONVICTION OF THE KILLER OF
WANDA WALKOWICZ

DID YOU SEE SOMETHING THAT MIGHT BE A CLUE, ON MONDAY
APRIL 2ND, 1973 AFTER 5 P.M. THINK !!!

* A SUSPICIOUS MAN OR CAR.
* A LITTLE RED HAIRED GIRL GETTING INTO A CAR WITH A MAN
  ON CONKEY, AVENUE'S 8 OR D.
* AN ACQUAINTANCE OR RELATIVE ACTING IN AN UNUSUAL MANNER ABOUT
  THIS TIME.
* A DISCARDED BAG OF GROCERIES.

WANDA DISAPPEARED FROM HER NEIGHBORHOOD ABOUT 5:30 P.M. MONDAY, APRIL 2,
1973, WHILE WALKING HOME WITH A LARGE BAG OF GROCERIES. DO YOU KNOW
ANYTHING ABOUT HER ABDUCTION OR MURDER?

BE A SECRET WITNESS - BEFORE IT HAPPENS AGAIN, PLEASE CONTACT:
CITIZENS FOR A DECENT COMMUNITY
P.O. BOX 9796
ROCHESTER, NEW YORK 14623

NO CLUE IS TOO SMALL. SHOW THIS TO YOUR FRIENDS. TALK ABOUT IT. NO CHILD IS
SAFE. THE MAN WHO COMMITTED THIS CRIME NEEDS HELP. WE WILL GET IT FOR HIM.
IF YOU WANT TO TALK TO SOMEONE ABOUT THIS, CALL SECRET WITNESS LINE 436-
2213. AN OFFICER OF THE C.D.C. WILL SPEAK TO YOU AND KEEP YOUR IDENTITY
SECRET.

`12.1`

WANTED BY THE FBI

INTERSTATE FLIGHT - MURDER

THEODORE ROBERT BUNDY

DESCRIPTION

6, Burlington, Vermont (not supported by birth records); Height, 5'11" to
pounds; Build, slender, athletic; Hair, dark brown, collar length; Eyes, blue;
ow; Race, white; Nationality, American; Occupations, bellboy, busboy,
her, janitor, law school student, office worker, political campaign worker,
ker, salesman, security guard; Scars and Marks, mole on neck, scar on
Number used, 533-44-4655; Remarks, occasionally stammers when upset;
se mustache and beard as disguise in past; left-handed; can imitate British
ysical fitness and health enthusiast.

CRIMINAL RECORD
Bundy has been convicted of aggravated kidnapping.

CAUTION

LEGE - EDUCATED PHYSICAL FITNESS ENTHUSIAST WITH A PRIOR
PE, IS BEING SOUGHT AS A PRISON ESCAPEE AFTER BEING CONVICTED
ND WHILE AWAITING TRIAL INVOLVING A BRUTAL SEX SLAYING OF A
RESORT. HE SHOULD BE CONSIDERED ARMED, DANGEROUS AND AN

`13.1`

13. Bundy Wanted

On December 30, 1977, while incarcerated and facing murder charges, Ted Bundy slipped out of a hole he had carved in the ceiling of his Colorado jail cell after purposely losing 25 pounds. While on the run, Bundy killed at least three more women, including a 12-year-old girl. On February 15, 1978, Bundy was recaptured and went to trial in 1979, where he was convicted of multiple counts of kidnapping and murder.

`13.1` During Bundy's time on the run, these wanted posters were displayed in post offices and police stations across the country. His description reads: "Occasionally stutters when upset, has worn glasses, false mustache and beard as disguise in the past ... can imitate British accent."

'Ted Bundy slipped out of a hole he had carved in the ceiling of his Colorado jail cell after purposely losing 25 pounds.'

ILLINOIS STATE PENITENTIARY
Joliet, Illinois

NAME ___ Richard Franklin Speck ___ Classification ___

REF. _Death 10-5-91_

RIGHT HAND

3. R. MIDDLE FINGER   4. R. RING FINGER   5. R. LITTLE FINGER

LEFT HAND

8. L. MIDDLE FINGER   9. L. RING FINGER   10. L. LITTLE FINGER

RIGHT HAND

JOLIET, ILL. DATE   APR 11 1973

IMPRESSIONS TAKEN BY
CLASSIFIED BY

PRISONER'S SIGNATURE _Richard Speck_

ILLINOIS STATE PENITENTIARY
Joliet, Illinois

Name   Richard Franklin Speck   Reg. No.   61114
Alias   Color   White
Crime   Murder   County   La Salle
Sentence   Death
Convicted   73
Remarks

Age   Weight
Nationality   Height
Build
Birthplace   Complexion
Occupation   Hair
Education   Color of Eyes

Scars, Marks, etc.

Criminal History

14. Born to Raise Hell

Two days after Richard Speck murdered eight student nurses in 1966, he attempted suicide in his room at the Starr Hotel in Chicago. Speck was taken to Cook County Hospital, where a physician recognized the "Born to Raise Hell" tattoo that the press had reported was on the killer's arm. Speck was convicted at trial and sentenced to death, but this was later overturned and the sentence changed to 1,200 years. Speck died of a heart attack in 1991.

14.1 Richard Speck-signed fingerprint card and mug shot from Illinois State Penitentiary, 1973.

15. Mother's Boy

Gary Mark Gilmore was a convicted murderer sentenced to death for two senseless murders. Over the course of two nights in July of 1976, he robbed and murdered Max Jensen, a gas station employee in Orem, Utah, and Bennie Bushnell, a motel manager in Provo. Despite both men complying with his demands, he killed them, ordering them to lie down and then shooting them in the back of the head, execution style.

15.1 An in-prison snapshot of Gilmore and his mom.

16. Merry Christmas

In 1968, years before he would become one of America's most prolific serial killers, John Wayne Gacy was convicted of sodomizing 15-year-old Donald Vorhees and slapped with a ten-year sentence at Anamosa State Penitentiary. He was released in 1971 and shortly after married Carole Hoff, who had two young daughters from a previous marriage.

16.1 A Christmas greeting from this period shows Gacy as a regular family man. In the words of Sam Amirante, one of the lawyers who defended Gacy in his later murder trial: "That's the scariest thing about him … He was a little Santa Claus jolly-looking kind of guy."

15.1

16.1

Merry Christmas

The Gacy's

17.1

18.1

17. Printed Proof

Before DNA tracing or even the use of Luminol (the blood-detecting chemical utilized by crime scene technicians), fingerprint tracing was considered the height of forensic technology. Shown here is a nineteenth-century "murder kit" containing fingerprint-dusting materials.

17.1 **The powders would be lightly dusted over a surface in the hope that they would reveal latent fingerprints by adhering to sweat and oil from the perpetrators' hands, showing up ridge detail.**

18. Early Forensics

In the early days of forensic science, a host of experts emerged who made claims to be able to determine a person's guilt or how they were murdered, including being able to tell whether a person was a criminal by smelling them.

18.1 **This exhibit was used at trial in the late nineteenth century to prove that a victim had been poisoned with arsenic.**

19. A Fat Profit

Up until the nineteenth century in some parts of Europe, traditional medicine called for the use of human fat, which was believed to have magic healing properties. Some enterprising executioners harvested the fat from the dead bodies and sold it to be used in the manufacture of supposedly curative ointments. This was a significant source of revenue for many executioners.

19.1 **An eighteenth-century porcelain jar with the Latin words *Axungia hominis*, which translates to "soft human fat."**

20. Captain Miller

In 1933 Captain Johan Eric Miller was found dead and stuffed into a canvas seabag in Lake Union. In addition to being shot in the head, he had been stabbed with a butcher's knife, robbed, and thrown in the lake while still alive.

20.1 **A double-sleeved evidence envelope describes some vitals about the murder, the victim, and the people in charge. It also holds the small-caliber slug taken from Miller's head.**

THE VAMPIRE OF PARIS

F rance has had its share of high-profile murderers, going as far back as 1440 with the nobleman Gilles de Rais, a leader in the French army and a companion-in-arms to Joan of Arc. After de Rais was finally arrested, it was determined he had killed over 140 people, primarily children. He was also suspected of taking part in satanic rituals and making pacts with the devil.

More recent killers to grab the French headlines include "the Poisoner of Chambéry," a nurse's aide who poisoned elderly people using antidepressants; "the Marseille Ripper," who kidnapped, raped, and murdered three sex workers and a student in Marseille; and "the Vampire of Paris," a self-proclaimed practicing satanist, who in November 1994 was arrested for the ritual killing of Thierry Bissonnier. "The Vampire of Paris" eventually confessed to the crime, was convicted, and ultimately served six years of a 12-year sentence for the murder.

Nico Claux—artist, author, morgue attendant, and true crime collector—is "the Vampire of Paris." As such, his high profile within the true crime community has led to some unique offers. "In 2004, I was living in Sweden, and Issei Sagawa wanted to be eaten alive by my girlfriend. He sent me dozens of paintings. Some to keep and others to sell so I could buy him a one-way ticket to Sweden. Customs seized the box, and they asked me to pay a ridiculous fee to release the package. I had to refuse, and it was sent back to him. He assumed I was upset, so he stopped writing, much to the relief of my girlfriend, who was genuinely frightened of him. Five years later, Sagawa resurfaced via his agent, and we collaborated on several art projects."

Many true crime collectors are asked about the "ethics" of the practice. In Nico's case, because of his past and present, the question and sometimes the judgment goes far deeper. "Most people are outraged by the fact that I still breathe and live on this planet. But you know what? I love doing what I do, and I'm delighted with my life. All my life, I have been cast away for not bowing down to herd mentality. Life is not about good or evil; it's about survival. I give absolutely zero f***s about what people think of me."

The collection of Nico Claux

Nico's collection is a unique combination of items he has acquired or been given as gifts and pieces he has created himself. His entrée into the world of true crime collecting is a bit unusual, in that other people were sourcing his own artwork before he became a collector himself. While incarcerated, he wrote to fellow inmates to exchange experiences about prison life and kill time. He corresponded with over 30 convicted killers and ultimately wrote a book based on that correspondence called *Je tue donc je suis (I kill therefore I am)* under the pen name Nicolas Castelaux. "We would also exchange advice on collectors who could be trusted. Sometimes I would see my paintings offered on websites for ten times the price I had sold them for. It made me realize the value of the letters and artwork from other inmates I had gathered over the years."

"When I was released from prison in 2002, many so-called profilers and wannabe cyber sleuths claimed that I would soon be back in prison for other murders. Twenty years have passed, and I am still a free man. Over those 20 years, I have written seven books, including *The Cannibal Cookbook* and my autobiography *The Gospel of Blood*, and been kicked out of morgues because I organized satanic black masses in their chapels."

Photos by Alexandre Halbardier

1.1

1. Killed on a Coffin

In 2001 Manuela Ruda, along with her then husband Daniel Ruda, stabbed Frank Hackert 66 times on a coffin that he and his wife used as a coffee table at their home in Bochum, Germany. They both admitted to drinking his blood after they killed him. Daniel and Manuela testified they had chosen Hackert for their sacrifice because he was "so funny and would be the perfect court jester for Satan."

Daniel was sentenced to 16 years in jail for the murder, and Manuela to 13 years. Nico has kept up a ten-year correspondence with Manuela that started while she was still in prison and continued after she was released. She has since changed her name and keeps a very low profile.

1.1 An unusual gift of a mummified bird head, which was given to Nico by convicted killer Manuela Ruda.

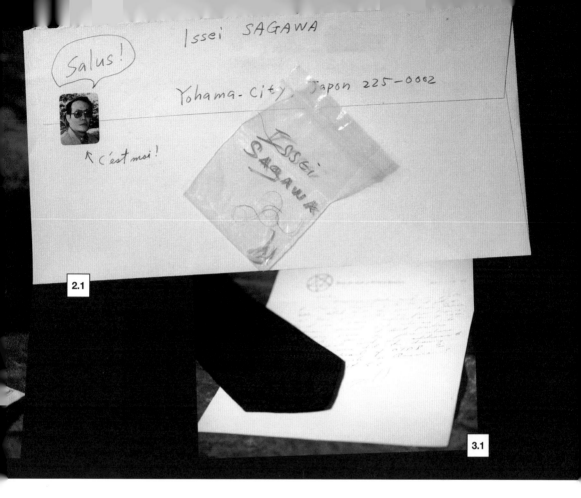

2. Murderer, Cannibal, Free Man

Japanese murderer, cannibal, and necrophile Issei Sagawa is known for killing Renée Hartevelt in Paris in 1981. At just 4 foot 9 inches tall, Sagawa stated in post-murder interviews that he considered himself weak, ugly, and small, and that by killing and eating Hartevelt he could absorb her strength and energy. Released on a technicality, he is now a free man living in his home country of Japan.

2.1 Nico has been corresponding with Issei Sagawa for over a decade. Their pen-pal friendship has garnered Nico a multitude of Sagawa items, including artwork, along with very personal items such as the pubic hair and fingernails shown here.

3. A Satanic Necktie

Nico has a fascination with Richard "the Night Stalker" Ramirez, and has the black necktie that Ramirez had worn in court in his collection. Sold to Nico by Ramirez's ex-wife, Doreen Ramirez, Nico would actually wear this tie while he was working in morgues.

3.1 Displayed beside the tie is the first letter that Ramirez sent to Nico in 1997, which clearly shows a Satanic pentagram symbol.

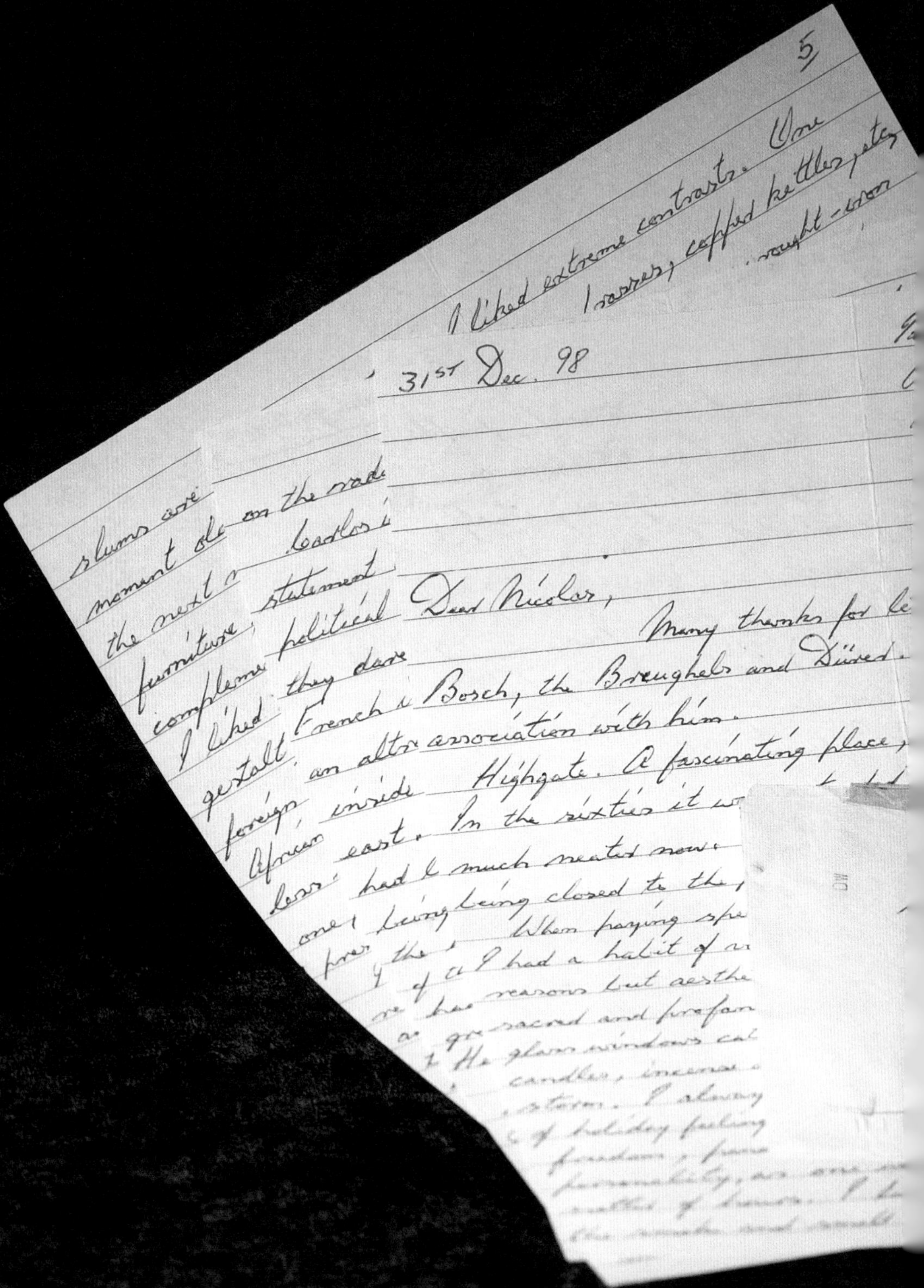

5

I liked extreme contrasts. One
[...] rasses, capped kettles jets,
[...] wrought-iron

31st Dec. 98

slums are
moment ole on the road
the next [...] Carlos i
furniture, statement
complexme political   Dear Nicolas,
I liked they dare   Many thanks for le[...]
gestalt French i Bosch, the Breughels and Dürer.
foreign, an altr association with him.
African, inside   Highgate. A fascinating place,
less, east. In the sixties it wo[...]
one, had I much neater now.
fres, the, being closed to the [...]
[...] y the, When paying spe[...]
of it I had a habit of [...]
[...] re has reasons but aesthe[...]
[...] a gre sacred and profan
[...] the glass windows cal
[...] candles, incense [...]
[...] storm. I always
[...] of holiday feeling
[...] freedom, fine
[...] formality, as one [...]
[...] matter of humour. I b[...]
[...] the smoke and smell

4.1

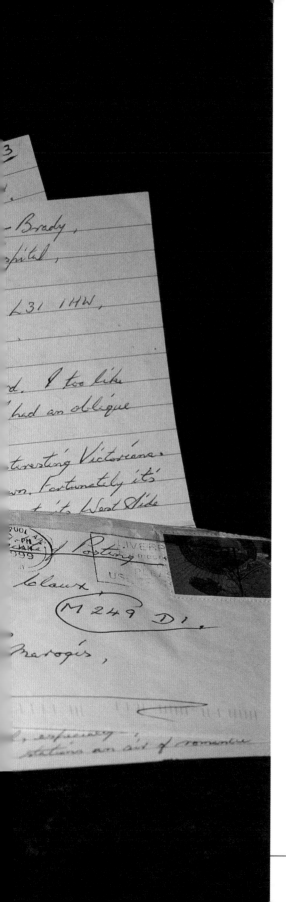

4. Letter from a Moors Murderer

Between July 1963 and October 1965, Ian Brady and Myra Hindley sexually assaulted and murdered five children, both boys and girls, in and around Manchester, England. These killings became known as the Moors Murders and received worldwide attention. When the pair were apprehended and ultimately brought to trial, the judge, Mr. Justice Fenton Atkinson, described Brady and Hindley as "two sadistic killers of the utmost depravity" in his closing remarks.

Both Hindley and Brady were convicted and sentenced to life imprisonment in 1966. Following his conviction, Brady spent 19 years at HM Prison Durham, where he asked to live in solitary confinement. In November of 1985, he was diagnosed as a psychopath and moved to the high-security Park Lane psychiatric hospital (later becoming Ashworth Hospital), from where he insisted he never wanted to be released.

Although Brady refused to cooperate with Ashworth's psychiatrists, he corresponded with people outside the hospital.

4.1 A handwritten letter from Ian Brady to Nico Claux, sent from Ashworth psychiatric hospital in 1998, while Nico was serving time for his own crimes. Brady discusses art, writing "I too like Bosch, the Breughels and Dürer," and says he had "an oblique association" with John Wayne Gacy. He also mentions Highgate Cemetery, calling it "a fascinating place with very interesting Victoriana."

'Although Brady refused to cooperate with Ashworth's psychiatrists, he corresponded with people outside the hospital.'

5.1

5. Nico Claux Gallery

On November 15, 1994, officers of the Parisian Brigade criminelle arrested the then 22-year-old Nicolas Claux outside the world-famous Moulin Rouge cabaret on suspicion of the murder of 34-year-old Thierry Bissonnier.

"Following my arrest, I was taken back to the Parisian Crime Department for questioning," says Nico. "Unbeknownst to me, crime scene investigators were already in the process of exercising a search warrant on my apartment. Inside they found a .22-caliber handgun under my bed, which they immediately sent off for ballistics tests. While they were probably not surprised to have found the pistol, they were almost certainly not prepared for the grisly scene that welcomed them. Throughout my apartment, bone fragments and human teeth were scattered about like loose change; vertebrae and leg bones hung from the ceiling like morbid mobiles, and hundreds of video cassettes, mostly slasher and hardcore S&M flicks, filled my shelves. One can only imagine what went through the minds of the investigators as they looked around my living quarters ... In addition to my tastes and choice of decor, investigators also discovered several stolen blood bags inside my refrigerator."

Nico confessed to Bissonnier's murder. Although the investigators were pleased to have solved the murder, they were deeply concerned with the human remains found in his apartment, and the blood bags in his refrigerator. "With little hesitation on my part, I informed them that I had been robbing the graves of several Parisian gothic graveyards and mutilating the mummified remains. When asked the reason why I was storing stolen blood bags inside my refrigerator, I simply answered that I drank the blood on a regular basis. Working as a mortuary assistant for ten months, I had been using my position as a means to fulfill a lifelong fantasy of mine revolving around cannibalism. When left alone to stitch the bodies after the autopsies, I would cut strips of meat from the ribs and eat them. On some occasions, I would bring pieces of flesh back to my place, where I would cook and eat those pieces as well."

5.1 An acrylic painting of the demon Kali, created by Nico Claux to illustrate the Death card of the Luciferian Tarot.

5.2 Acrylic paintings by Nico, based on mug shots of Charles Manson and Ted Bundy, and splattered with the artist's own blood.

5.3 Charcoal and acrylic self-portrait alongside Nico's portrait of Japanese serial killer Tsutomu Miyazaki.

5.2

THE VAMPIRE OF PARIS

239942

N. Claux

N. Claux

5.3

6. Ice Cold Killer

Armin Meiwes achieved international infamy in 2001 for killing and eating a man, whom he had found via an Internet cannibal fetish website and who volunteered to be killed and consumed.

Over a period of ten months he proceeded to dismember and eat the corpse, storing the body parts in his freezer, refrigerator, and in pizza boxes. He eventually consumed almost 44 pounds of flesh before he was arrested.

Meiwes was originally sentenced to eight-and-a-half years for manslaughter but was retried in 2006, at which time a psychologist declared that he could reoffend as Meiwes "still had fantasies about devouring the flesh of young people." While in prison, Meiwes has since become a vegetarian and, based on his previous involvement with the cannibal fetish community, he believes there are 800 active cannibals in Germany at any given time.

6.1 Nico found the fridge, freezer, and torture instruments in Meiwes's abandoned mansion. The items still bear the police stickers. At the time of writing, the freezer is up for sale on the Murder Auction website for $66,000.

7. Killer Ouija Board

This is one of the custom boards Nico has created and offered for sale on his site for $666. This board includes fibers from an article of clothing from Richard Ramirez, chips from Ted Bundy's Volkswagen, particles from Gerard Schaefer's ring, and grave dirt from Ed Gein's Plainsfield, Wisconsin, cemetery plot.

7.1 Portraits of the four murderers are at each corner, and Nico's own blood is smeared on the board.

'Nico found the fridge, freezer, and torture instruments in Meiwes's abandoned mansion.'

6.1

7.1

THIS DEATH HEAD RING
IS MY GIFT TO Nico CLAUX.
IT WAS GIVEN TO ME
BY GERARD JOHN SCHAEFER,
"THE SERIAL KILLER WHO
LOVED ME," WHEN I
VISITED HIM AT BELLE
GLADE PRISON IN FLORIDA
IN 1990. I BELIEVE HE
WOULD BE DELIGHTED
TO KNOW I FOUND HIS
RING SUCH A GOOD Home.
Sondra Honan 9/24/50

9.1

8. Ring of Death

Although only convicted of two murders and imprisoned in 1973 for the crimes, the one-time Florida sheriff's deputy Gerard Schaefer is suspected of up to seven more killings and has confessed to murdering more than 30 women.

In December 1995, Schaefer was stabbed to death in his prison cell. His sister Sara told reporters that Schaefer's murder was a cover-up related to his attempts to verify the confession made (and subsequently retracted) by Ottis Toole to the killing of Adam Walsh.

8.1 Gerard Schaefer gave this ring to his former girlfriend, Sondra London, during a prison visit in 1990. He told her it had belonged to another serial killer he had met in prison (suspected to be Ottis Toole or Gerald Stano). Sondra later gifted it to Nico, saying Gerard would have been "delighted to know I found his ring such a good home."

9. Friends or Fiends

Nico passed some of his time in prison corresponding with other notorious prisoners from around the world.

9.1 Left to right: David Gore, Bård "Faust" Eithun, Bobby Joe Long, Herbert Mullin, Richard Ramirez, Natasha Cornett, Doug Clark, Ángel Reséndiz, and Henry Lee Lucas.

To Rob. *John W. Gacy*
10-10-93

A PERSONAL CONNECTION

Throughout incarceration, there are times when a prisoner's access to paints, crayons, or colored pencils will be taken away due to an in-prison breach of conduct. During these periods inmates will often employ DIY measures to continue creating their artwork. An exhibition held in Los Angeles, California, displayed art created using "inks" made from melted chess pieces, soot, and fruit-flavored drinks. A curious comment made by many of the featured artists was that they had never drawn until they were incarcerated and never drew again after they got out.

Inmates cannot rely on receiving more art materials from outside, as sending mail to and from most federal lockups comes with a stringent set of rules. When pen pals, relatives, and friends correspond with prisoners via "snail mail," they must be mindful not to use staples or paper clips, as these seemingly benign items can easily be made into weapons by the inmates, and the letter will be returned to the sender.

The use of markers, crayons, glitter, glue, stickers, or lipstick on the letter or the envelope is also prohibited since it becomes a way to smuggle in drugs. Any drawings or markings that can be interpreted as secret code will be returned to sender, and you should never write anything in a letter that you wouldn't want seen by a third party: all mail is inspected and read by staff.

Much of Robert Webb's collection has resulted from him cultivating relationships by corresponding with over 350 inmates, along with personal visits to their penal institutions. He feels the need to know the source of each piece he holds and takes the time to write to the prisoner directly to develop the relationship, eventually receiving items or artwork via the inmates themselves. When asked if he felt any connection with the inmates he corresponds with, Robert said: "I considered my relationship with Roy [Norris] as that of a big brother ... while Art [Arthur Shawcross] was my uncle, and both wrote me as such. I miss those two a great deal."

The collection of Robert Webb

It was via an avid book collector that Robert was led into the world of true crime. In the 1990s he came upon a book documenting the life of John Wayne Gacy. Robert was fascinated by the polarity of Gacy, his ability to manage day-to-day life while literally knee-deep in his murderous ways. "I had read the book but was curious to hear his side of the story. So, I reached out to Gacy via mail, and he responded to my letter! Well, it wasn't actually a letter. It was a form for me to fill out about myself. I responded with a letter asking him to do the same for me. A few years later, I had the opportunity to obtain Gacy paintings directly from his dealer for $100 or less, depending on my choice. Unfortunately, I didn't take advantage of the offer."

Pieces that Robert is presently on the lookout for include a document signed by the nineteenth-century American serial killer H.H. Holmes. He would also love to make up for a past mistake of passing on an original copy of *Killer Fiction*, a compilation of Gerard Schaefer short stories and drawings, published by Sondra London in 1990 after she interviewed Schaefer following his conviction. "I try to keep an open mind as to the next piece I would like to add to my collection; however, I draw the line at pubic hair. That will not find its way into my collection."

Photos by Dan Howell

1.1

1. A Monster's Best Friend

There wasn't much joy for convicted murderer Henry Lee Lucas as a young child. Born in 1936 and raised in a one-room log cabin in Blacksburg, Virginia, his mother was a prostitute who would force her son to watch her engaging in sex with clients. She would also make him cross-dress in public, purportedly so she could later pimp him out to men and women. In addition, Lucas lost an eye at the age of ten when it became infected after a fight with his brother. In December 1949, Lucas's alcoholic father died of hypothermia after heading home drunk and collapsing outside during a blizzard.

1.1 A painting by Henry Lee Lucas of his childhood pet dog, which he said was the only thing he cared about as a child. Lucas's initials are on the plant pot.

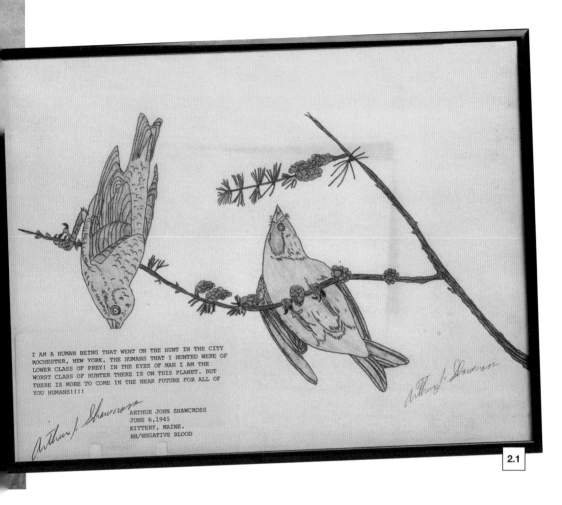

I AM A HUMAN BEING THAT WENT ON THE HUNT IN THE CITY
ROCHESTER, NEW YORK. THE HUMANS THAT I HUNTED WERE OF
LOWER CLASS OF PREY! IN THE EYES OF MAN I AM THE
WORST CLASS OF HUNTER THERE IS ON THIS PLANET. BUT
THERE IS MORE TO COME IN THE NEAR FUTURE FOR ALL OF
YOU HUMANS!!!!

ARTHUR JOHN SHAWCROSS
JUNE 6,1945
KITTERY, MAINE.
RH/NEGATIVE BLOOD

2.1

2. The Worst Hunter

Arthur Shawcross was a man of contradictions and conflicting stories. He claimed to have seen heavy combat and cannibalized two women while serving in Vietnam and this is what drove him to kill somewhere in the range of 13 to 53 people when he returned to the United States. However, an investigation into Shawcross reports that he saw no combat, but served as a clerk.

Chillingly, in the above frame, Shawcross's typed message reads "I am a human being that went on the hunt in the city of Rochester, New York." At his trial, the defense called forensic psychiatrist Dr. Dorothy Lewis to testify that Shawcross assumed an alternate personality named "Bessie" when he murdered his victims. She argued that Shawcross should be institutionalized, not imprisoned; however, Shawcross was sentenced to 250 years' incarceration.

2.1 | A pencil drawing and message where Shawcross declares himself to be "the worst class of hunter there is on this planet."

'I am a human being that went on the hunt in the city of Rochester, New York.'

3. A Deadly Business

Prolific as a killer—with 33 victims—John Wayne Gacy was a busy inmate when it came to producing works of art, most notably his "Pogos." He also spent a lot of time writing to pen pals, entertaining guests, and making collect calls to new-found friends on the outside. Much of his socializing skill came from his experience as a member of the Chamber of Commerce, as a charity volunteer playing Pogo the clown, and soliciting business for his contracting company. Handing out business cards to young men with the offer of a job, many times they would wind up dead and buried in the crawl space of his house.

3.1 A John Wayne Gacy-signed P.D.M. Contractors Corp. business card, along with a signed picture of Gacy and Robert Webb taken at Menard Correctional Center.

4. Strangler in the Night

Tall, dark, and handsome, Albert DeSalvo was charming and had a way with women. Unfortunately, his "way" often ended up with the women being strangled to death.

While Albert "the Boston Strangler" DeSalvo was serving a life sentence he was offered $50 for the rights to use his name and snippets from a prison-taped interview made by an attorney. These snippets were to be used in a parody of the Sinatra song "Strangers in the Night," entitled "Strangler in the Night." Totally tasteless.

4.1 A 45 rpm 7-inch vinyl record with an illustrated sleeve and a facsimile of Albert DeSalvo's signature. The A-side track is "Strangler in the Night" by Albert DeSalvo. The B-side track is "Albert, Albert" by The Bugs, produced by Astor Records in 1967.

3.1

"... These are my thoughts, feelings and emotions."

Albert H. De Salvo

STRANGLER IN THE NIGHT

Productions, Inc.
Cambridge, Massachusetts

4.1

5. The Tool Box Killers

When Lawrence Bittaker and Roy Norris met in California Men's Colony prison in 1977, they realized they had two common interests: sexual violence and misogyny. Two years later, having been released, Bittaker and Norris killed their first victim, 16-year-old Lucinda Lynn Schaefer, on June 24, 1979. That was the beginning of the Tool Box Killings. By the time the pair were arrested on November 20, 1979, they had raped and murdered five young girls, brutally torturing their victims with pliers, hammers, and ice picks.

While incarcerated, both men pointed the finger of blame at one another. Although Norris calmly admitted that he enjoyed having sex with their victims, he claimed only Bittaker enjoyed the acts of torture and murder, stating, "I didn't enjoy killing—that was Lawrence. It was his favorite part: watching the women struggle."

On December 13, 2019, at the age of 79, Bittaker died while incarcerated on San Quentin State Prison's death row. His death was reported as being due to natural causes.

On February 24, 2020, at the age of 72, Norris died of natural causes at the California Medical Facility associated with the Richard J. Donovan Correctional Facility.

> **5.1** A Norris and Bittaker collage including a signed photo of Bittaker, a photo of the collector with Roy Norris on a visit before Norris passed away, postcards adorned with Roy's art, and a court evidence photo of Roy.

> **5.2** A diverse selection of Roy Norris letters and envelope art.

> **5.3** Norris made this self-portrait and sent it directly to Robert with his signature and fingerprint. [Over the page.]

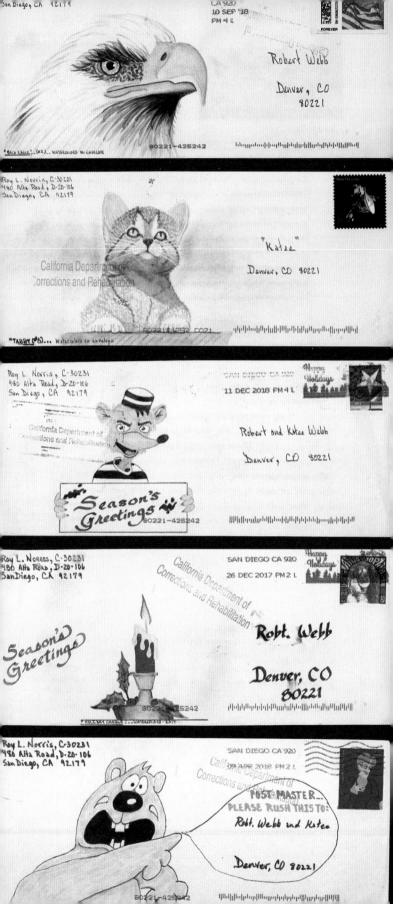

Robert--- Not as good a rendering of
myself as Tom's original, but I'm
getting better, month by month.

5.3

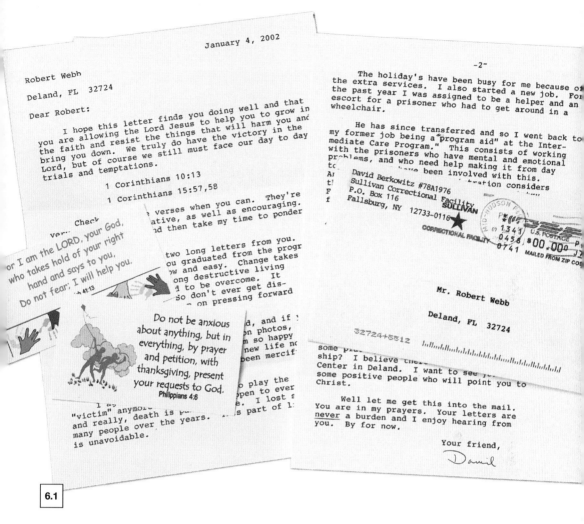

January 4, 2002

Robert Webb

Deland, FL 32724

Dear Robert:

I hope this letter finds you doing well and that you are allowing the Lord Jesus to help you to grow in the faith and resist the things that will harm you and bring you down. We truly do have the victory in the Lord, but of course we still must face our day to day trials and temptations.

1 Corinthians 10:13

1 Corinthians 15:57,58

Check ... verses when you can. They're ... ative, as well as encouraging. ... nd then take my time to ponder

or I am the LORD, your God,
who takes hold of your right
hand and says to you,
Do not fear; I will help you.
— 41:13

two long letters from you. ... ou graduated from the progr ... ow and easy. Change takes ... ong destructive living ... d to be overcome. It ... so don't ever get dis- ... on pressing forward

Do not be anxious
about anything, but in
everything, by prayer
and petition, with
thanksgiving, present
your requests to God.
Philippians 4:6

d, and if ... n photos, ... m so happy ... new life no ... been mercif ... o play the ... pen to ever ... e. I lost s ... s part of l:

"victim" anymor ... and really, death is p ... many people over the years. is unavoidable.

-2-

The holiday's have been busy for me because of the extra services. I also started a new job. For the past year I was assigned to be a helper and an escort for a prisoner who had to get around in a wheelchair.

He has since transferred and so I went back to my former job being a "program aid" at the Intermediate Care Program." This consists of working with the prisoners who have mental and emotional problems, and who need help making it from day to ... A ... ve been involved with this. ... ration considers
David Berkowitz #78A1976
Sullivan Correctional Facility
P.O. Box 116
Fallsburg, NY 12733-0116

Mr. Robert Webb

Deland, FL 32724

32724+5512

some pi... ship? I believe the... Center in Deland. I want to see y... some positive people who will point you to Christ.

Well let me get this into the mail. You are in my prayers. Your letters are never a burden and I enjoy hearing from you. By for now.

Your friend,

Daniel

6.1

6. Son of Hope

From the day David Berkowitz was arrested on August 10, 1977, until his present-day position of serving six life sentences at Shawangunk Correctional Facility for killing six people, the motive behind the Son of Sam murders is still not clear.

On arrest, Berkowitz claimed that a dog belonging to his neighbor was one of the reasons he killed, stating that the dog demanded the blood of pretty young girls. A few weeks later, he alluded to a tale of demonic possession and said: "There are other Sons out there; God help the world." Then, at a press conference in February 1979, Berkowitz declared that his previous claims of demonic possession were all a hoax.

In 1987 Berkowitz converted to evangelical Christianity. He stated that his moment of conversion came after reading Psalm 34:6 from a Bible gifted to him by another inmate. It was after this conversion that Berkowitz said he is no longer to be referred to as the "Son of Sam" but rather the "Son of Hope."

6.1 A scripture-riddled letter from David Berkowitz to the collector, along with religious notecards he has sent.

'There are other Sons out there; God help the world.'

7. Personal Study Bible

The Bible plays an integral part in the teachings of all Christian-based congregations. David Koresh's sect of Branch Davidians concentrated on the beliefs found in the Book of Revelation, also called the Apocalypse of John, the Apocalypse of Jesus Christ, and the Book of Apocalypse. This is the last book of the Bible, which predicts apocalyptic events leading up to the return of Jesus Christ. Branch Davidians believed that the judgments of the Last Prophesy were about to be realized.

Allegations of Koresh's involvement in multiple incidents of physical and sexual abuse of children led the Bureau of Alcohol, Tobacco, and Firearms to finally plan the siege on the sect's Waco compound that ended in tragedy.

7.1 This was the personal study bible of Lois Roden, the wife of Benjamin Roden who founded the Branch Davidians. Lois gave it to the collector's brother to encourage him to attend services there. Handwritten notes reveal the birth of the cult while marking out the actual scripture to correspond with their beliefs. They give an important insight into the mind of someone in a cult: it all comes down to a matter of interpretation.

7.2 A photo of the compound taken while Robert was at Waco. Note the banner, "Rodney King, We Understand," which was dropped out of the window during the siege, indicating that the inhabitants understood what it was like to be persecuted by the State.

'Branch Davidians believed that the judgments of the Last Prophesy were about to be realized.'

7.1

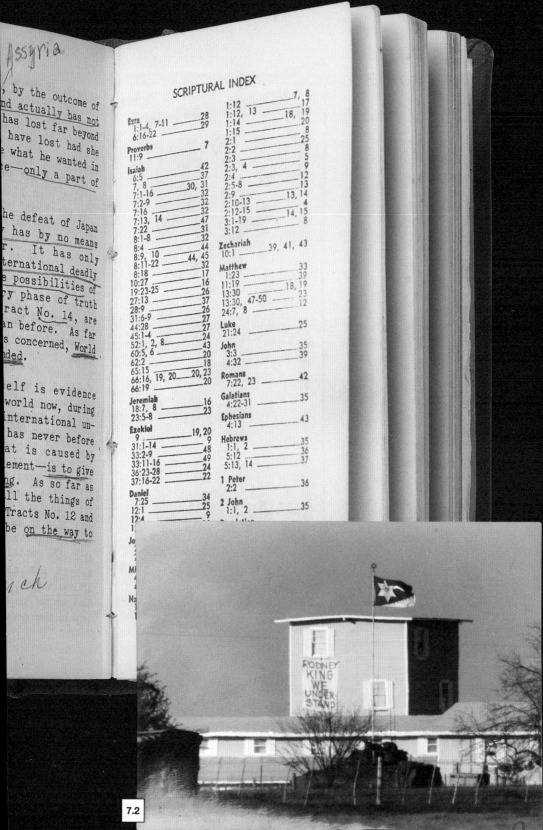

7.2

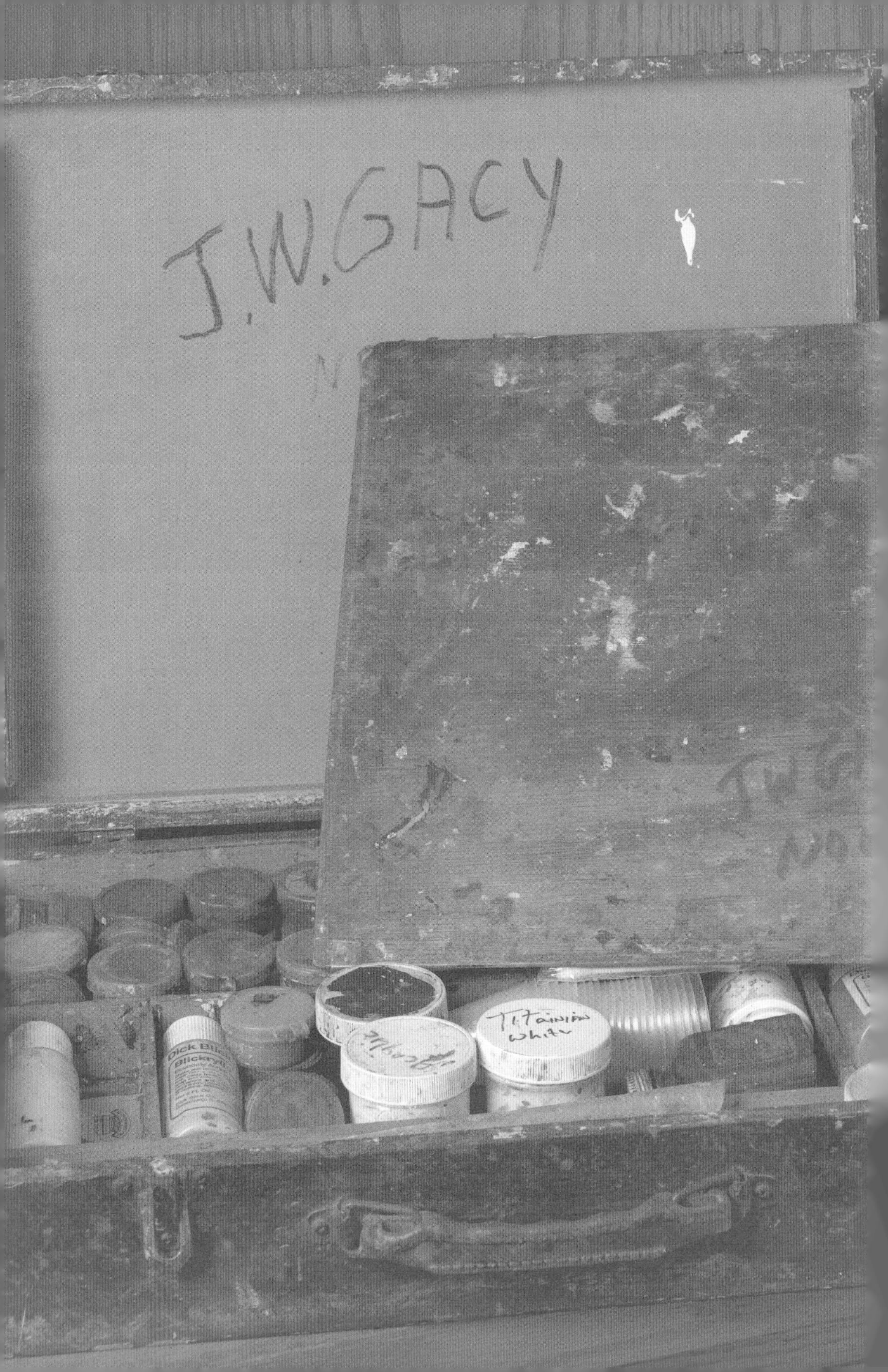
J.W.GACY

THE PSYCHOLOGY OF SERIAL KILLING

Fans of the popular Netflix series *Mindhunter* will know it was back in the 1970s that Robert Ressler, an FBI agent, played a significant role in the psychological profiling of violent offenders. Ressler has often been credited with coining the term "serial killer," but in fact that is a direct translation of the German *Serienmörder*, coined in 1930 by Ernst Gennat, a Berlin police investigator. Gennat has also been immortalized on film as the fictional Inspector Karl Lohmann, who first appeared in Fritz Lang's *M* (1931) and *The Testament of Dr. Mabuse* (1932).

As the author of *The Psychopathology of Serial Murder: A Theory of Violence* (1996) and *Real-Life Monsters: A Psychological Examination of the Serial Murderer* (2012), Stephen Giannangelo has come face to face with many serial killers, and his general interest in collecting led to the curating of a fine true crime collection. "I've always been a bit of a collector, and after I started studying Forensic Psychology in grad school, I became fascinated by the overlap of clinical study of items like letters and paintings by deeply disturbed criminals. The psychology and the analysis of these items tell a story you cannot get in a book or even in a structured interview."

No discussion of the psychology of serial killers is complete without mentioning John Wayne Gacy, and it is him that Stephen's collection is centered around. In addition to being infamous for his murderous exploits, Gacy also holds the distinction of being one of the most sought-after inmate artists, with his paintings realizing price tags in the thousands. Many believe that Gacy's Pogo paintings are the most iconic images in true crime collecting. Although Stephen is in possession of one of the most sought-after items related to Gacy, his collection is not simply focused on Gacy's paintings and Pogo, but also around Gacy himself as the creator. Stephen approaches his acquisitions with the philosophy, "If the art or letters do not support any educational value, I don't want them."

The collection of Stephen J. Giannangelo

Not many people can say that a chance meeting with Alfred Hitchcock as a child had a significant influence on their decision to become a true crime collector. But that meeting instilled in the young Stephen a preoccupation with horror. Later, on discovering that monsters, such as Charles Manson, really existed, his interests gravitated to abnormal psychology and crime.

Stephen's first serious purchase also had a unique twist to it. He purchased a Gacy Pogo painting to use as a teaching tool in one of his university classes, which proved to be a wild success as a discussion starter. Since then Stephen's collection has grown and now includes one of the most sought-after items in true crime: John Wayne Gacy's art kit. "It's pretty special. I'm also rather partial to my Dahmer greeting cards and, of course, Pogo," says Stephen.

Stephen understands why people question the ethics of true crime collecting but insists: "I find the artifacts to be historical mementos. I'm not glorifying offenders, nor am I defending them. However, I do see a specific educational value. I also think, especially today, with all the partisan censorship and canceling and erasing of history, it's a very slippery slope when some people decide what others can read or study."

Photos by Dan Howell

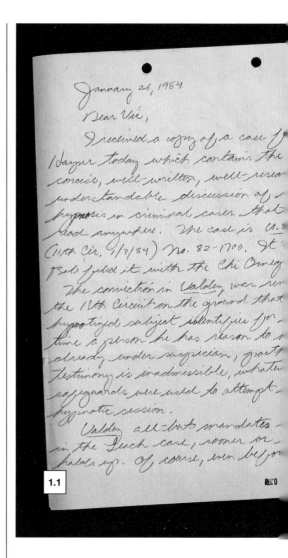

1.1   REC'D

1. Bundy Investigates

This letter was written by Ted Bundy to one of his last attorneys, Vic Africano, in 1984. During his appeal hearings Bundy continually called into question testimony given by witnesses under hypnosis at his trials. The letter's content is interesting, as Bundy quotes precedent and legal research on the admissibility of post-hypnotic testimony. This is an excellent example of Bundy being capable of contributing to his legal representation, demonstrating that it was not just a story or part of his legend.

1.1 Bundy refers to a case file that contains the most "well-researched and understandable discussion of hypnosis in criminal cases that I have found anywhere."

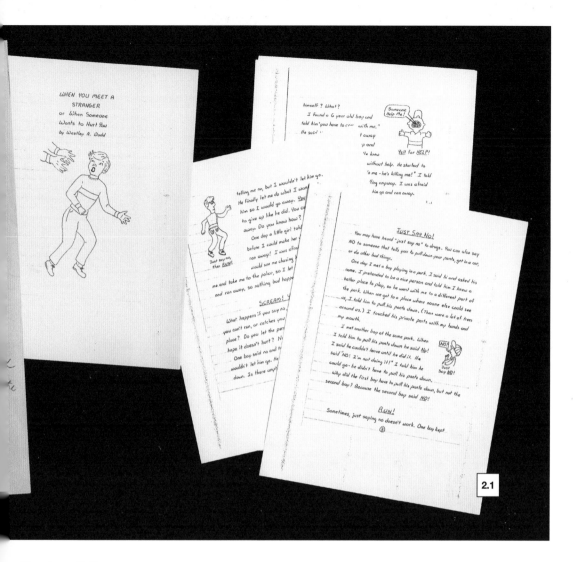

The handwritten brochure pages read in part:

WHEN YOU MEET A STRANGER
or When Someone
Wants to Hurt You
by Westley A. Dodd

Just say no,
then RUN!

himself? What?
I found a 6 year old boy and told him "you have to come with me."
He said...
...t away
...p and
...He knew
without help. He started to
...o me - he's killing me!" I told
...ling anyway. I was afraid
him go and ran away.

Someone Help Me!

Yell for HELP!

telling me no, but I wouldn't let him go.
He finally let me do what I wan...
him so I would give up like he did. You c...
to give up like he did. You ca...
away. Do you know how?
One day a little girl told...
before I could make her...
ran away! I was afra...
could see me chasing...
me and take me to the police, so I let...
and ran away, so nothing bad happ...

SCREAM! Y...

What happens if you say no...
you can't run, or catches you...
place? Do you let the pers...
hope it doesn't hurt? N...
One boy said no and t...
wouldn't let him go. He...
down. Is there anyth...

JUST SAY NO!

You may have heard "just say no" to drugs. You can also say
NO to someone that tells you to pull down your pants, get in a car,
or do other bad things.

One day I met a boy playing in a park, I said hi and asked his
name. I pretended to be a nice person and told him I knew a
better place to play, so he went with me to a different part of
the park. When we got to a place where noone else could see
us, I told him to pull his pants down. (There were a lot of trees
around us.) I touched his private parts with my hands and
my mouth.

I met another boy at the same park. When
I told him to pull his pants down he said No!
I said he couldn't leave until he did it. He
said "NO! I'm not doing it!" I told him he
could go - he didn't have to pull his pants down.
Why did the first boy have to pull his pants down, but not the
second boy? Because the second boy said NO!

NO!
Just
Say NO!

RUN!
Sometimes, just saying no doesn't work. One boy kept

3

2.1

2. Avoid the Monsters

In the summer of 1989, Westley Allan Dodd was only 28 years old but had already molested almost 50 young boys and been arrested multiple times on child molestation charges, each time only receiving short stints behind bars or court-mandated therapy. By the fall of 1989 Dodd had stepped up his game, and between September and October murdered three children: Dodd molested and killed two brothers, aged 10 and 11 years old, before abducting a four-year-old boy, bringing him back to his home where he molested and strangled the child, and then hung him in his closet.

Dodd was arrested in November 1989. He pleaded guilty and was given the death penalty. He refused to appeal against his death sentence, stating: "I must be executed before I have an opportunity to escape or kill someone else. If I do escape, I promise you I will kill and rape again, and I will enjoy every minute of it." He was hanged on January 5, 1993.

2.1 **A copy of the brochure created in prison by Westley Allan Dodd, ostensibly to warn and train parents, teachers, and children how to avoid monsters like him. He advises children to "just say no," to "yell for help," and to "run!" The collector was contacted in person by FBI agents at one point, asking where he had obtained this item.**

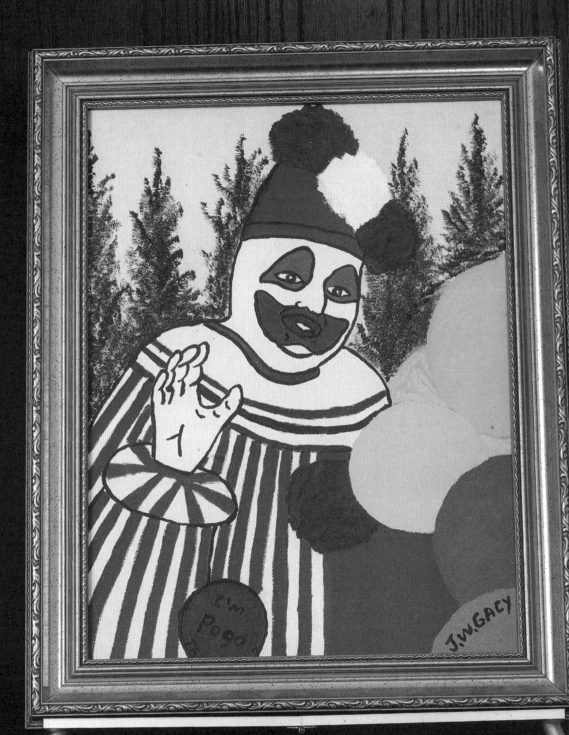

3.1

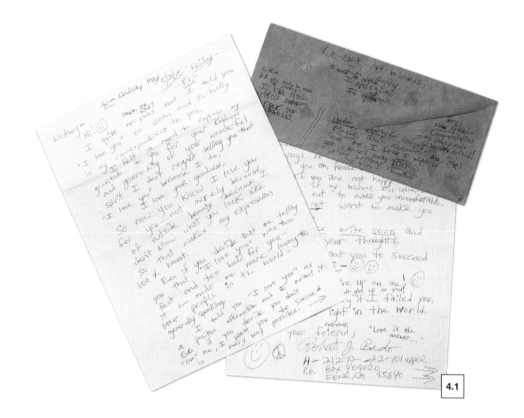

4.1

3. Goodbye Pogo

On December 21, 1978, John Wayne Gacy was in police custody, having just confessed to the torture, rape, and murder of 33 young men and boys. He was sitting in county lockup when the forensic team began to dig up the ground beneath the crawl space of Gacy's home in Chicago, Illinois. Within minutes, they had uncovered putrefied flesh and a human arm bone.

The self-portrait of serial killer John Wayne Gacy as Pogo the Clown is likely the most recognizable piece of true crime collector art. Also in Stephen's collection are three paintings from Gacy's "Hi-Ho" series, where he depicted the Seven Dwarfs from *Snow White* in various outdoor scenic situations. One of these, with imagery including little boys with digging tools heading out of an underground tunnel, has been the subject of endless speculation and analysis.

3.1 This piece is known as a "Goodbye Pogo," one of the last pieces Gacy made before his execution. Gacy reportedly made several of these to gift to close pen pals near the end of his life.

4. Lasting Obsession

Robert Bardo, stalker and murderer of the young actress Rebecca Schaeffer, doesn't waver from his propensity for obsession when it comes to pursuing a "potential lover." In this letter to a female pen pal he apologizes for telling her he loved her so soon, writing, "I felt a need to express my gratitude to you for your kindness and generosity of your wonderful spirit. I don't regret telling you that 'I love you' because I do." And on the envelope he continues, "I'm sorry, I apologize, I'm eccentric."

4.1 Pages from a letter written by Bardo give an insight into his obsessive and disordered thinking.

'Pogo the Clown is likely the most recognizable piece of true crime collector art.'

5. Happy Little Balloons

There are no accounts of Gacy having abducted, tortured, or killed any of his more than 33 victims while dressed as his characters Pogo or Patches, though it was reported that he would remain in his clown costume after a performance to grab a drink at a local bar before returning home. Nevertheless, one can't help but feel that Gacy creating his grinning Pogo and Patches paintings while sitting on death row at Menard Correctional Center in southern Illinois was a slap in the face to the families of those people he killed.

This art kit and box of watercolor paints and brushes was owned and used by John Wayne Gacy in the early 1990s. This is regarded as one of the most prized objects in the realm of true crime collecting.

5.1 The set is likely one of only two that exist, the other being at the Crime Museum in Pigeon Forge, Tennessee. It has several markings that identify it as Gacy's, including his name on the inside lid of the box and in several of the art books. Included are the sherbet lids Gacy used to trace many of the balloons featured in his most infamous Pogo paintings. A significant part of this item is the authentic paper trail of documentation that came with it, tracing the order from the art store to Gacy at Menard prison.

'Included are the sherbet lids Gacy used to trace many of the balloons featured in his most infamous Pogo paintings.'

5.1

MADISON WI 537
PM
24 OCT

10-23-94

My Dearest Barbara,
Hello, and how is my special
and most Beautiful friend? Thanks s
much for your card! I hope that thing
are still going well for you at sch
Did you know that my cell
"jumping" spiders in it? I killed
months ago. I don't like them
I'm afraid that one will crawl
my ear, or up my nose while I'm
sleeping! Oh well, soon winter will
here, and I won't have to worry about
creepy insects anymore.
The judge still hasn't deci
about my garnishment, This is the se
time that he's said he would, de
by a certain date, and then change
his mind. You can't even trust the
judges to stick by their word
these days! But at least the
has started to let me buy
week again. It's nice to be able
stamps, cigarettes, and coffee each
like the other inmates. The final
able to pay back the other inm
It was raining for most
yesterday. It finally stopped c
and I looked out my window
this Huge solid Pink rainbow
seen a Pink rainbow before.
Barbara, I love you, and
you in my thoughts and pray
OXOXOX ... !!!

6.1

6. Greetings from the Milwaukee Monster

While serving out his 941-year prison sentence in Wisconsin's Columbia Correctional Facility for the rape, murder, and cannibalism (sometimes not in that order) of 17 known victims, the "Milwaukee Monster" Jeffrey Dahmer found time to send greetings cards to his many pen pals. Although these cards appear innocuous, some contain references to a potential unknown murder perpetrated by Dahmer.

Dahmer was beaten to death in the prison bathroom by two inmates shortly after this letter was sent. His attorney later commented that Dahmer had always had a death wish, saying, "I know that he didn't have the gumption to do it himself, so I predicted that the day would come when he would be killed in prison."

> **6.1** Dahmer complains to a pen pal about the insects in his prison cell: "Did you know my cell has jumping spiders in it? I killed one two nights ago. I don't like them because I'm afraid that one will crawl into my ear or up my nose while I'm sleeping!"

'Dahmer was beaten to death in the prison bathroom by two inmates shortly after this letter was sent.'

...day...

...a day to dream on
...a day to enjoy
...a day to remember!

Happy Birthday !!!

My Dearest Barbara,
May your special day be filled with joy and every good thing.
all my love,
XOXOXO! and many ...

MADISON WI 53
PM
5
1994

04 05 94 DCR 241 #3 3MSM53?

50

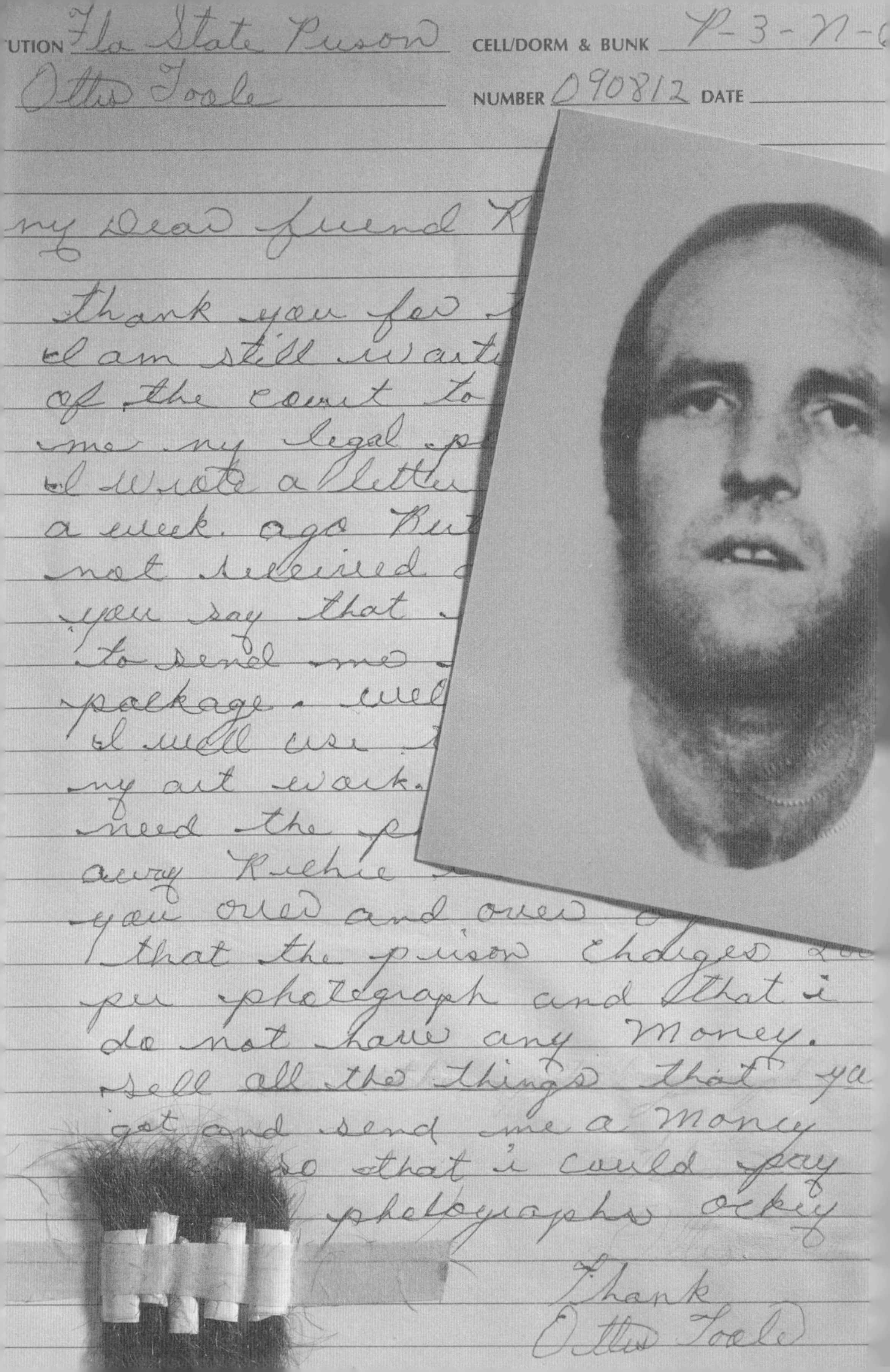

UTION **Fla State Prison** CELL/DORM & BUNK **P-3-N-6**

Ottis Toole NUMBER **090812** DATE _____

my Dear friend R_____

    Thank you for _____
I am still waiti____
of the court to ____
me my legal p____
I wrote a letter ____
a week ago But ____
not recieved ____
you say that ____
to send me ____
package. wel____
I will use ____
my art work.____
need the p____
away Richie ____
you owed and owed ____
that the prison charges ____
per photograph and that i
do not have any Money.
sell all the things that ya
get and send me a money
_____ so that i could pay
_____ photographs ockey

                    Thank
                Ottis Toole

SINCERELY YOURS

Why do people become obsessed with and write to serial killers and mass murderers? The knee-jerk reaction to that question is usually, "Oh, those people are just weirdos." Well, there are "weirdos" in every group, including people who collect teapots, so that's not the answer. It's suggested that there are three reasons why people reach out to those who have committed such heinous acts. Some are trying to understand something that they cannot comprehend: they cannot wrap their minds around how someone can be so evil. Others subconsciously feel that, if they know how a serial killer thinks, they will have a better chance of not becoming a victim of one. For the majority, it's a justification that, despite how evil the killers were, justice won out and they are safely behind bars.

The collection belonging to Dr. David Adamovich and Lynn Wheat consists of more than 30,000 pieces, primarily letters and photographs. David explains how they came into their possession: "We began 'collecting' in November 2018. But we are not the collectors. We purchased the collection in its entirety from a deceased friend. We consider ourselves the curators of what we call the 'Rosetta Collection' of serial killer murderabilia—so named because it was under wraps and its existence unknown for nearly 30 years."

The collection is partly displayed in their home, but the majority resides in 125 boxes and shipping crates housed in two storage facility lockers. The contents read like a who's who of infamous serial murders, but within those 30,000 pieces are lesser-known crimes with stories that are just as tragic, many dating back as far as the 1920s.

When the collection was purchased in its entirety by David and Lynn, their first task was to catalog and photograph or scan all 30,000+ pieces, a project that took over a year. Lynn read every letter in an effort to capture a serial killer's hidden gem among the endless banality. Her efforts were not in vain, and among the most memorable finds were Gacy's references to masturbation and eating his own semen, Arthur Shawcross's complete lack of remorse, Squeaky Fromme's confessed love for Charles Manson, and Richard Ramirez's continued sexual deviancy and bloodlust.

The collection of Dr. David R. Adamovich and Lynn J. Wheat

As you approach David and Lynn's beautiful waterfront home, it's not the view of Long Island Sound that captures your attention: it's the "wheel of death" that sits in their driveway. David Adamovich, better known as The Great Throwdini, is officially the fastest knife thrower in the world and has set or broken 36 Guinness World Records. His partner Lynn is Throwdini's official "target girl."

David and Lynn purchased their entire collection of over 30,000 pieces in one fell swoop, including a bunk bed from the California-based UFO religious cult, Heaven's Gate. Already in possession of one of the largest on record, it's no surprise that they are not looking to expand their collection. Since their overnight high-profile appearance in the true crime collecting world, David and Lynn have been offered many items but have declined everything. They prefer to keep the collection as is, not adding to it, but maybe selling off a few individual pieces to collectors. "However, one piece in our possession that we will never sell is a lock of hair from Ted Bundy." This hair was shaved from his head just prior to his execution and obtained from his death row associate G.J. Schaefer.

Photos by Dan Howell

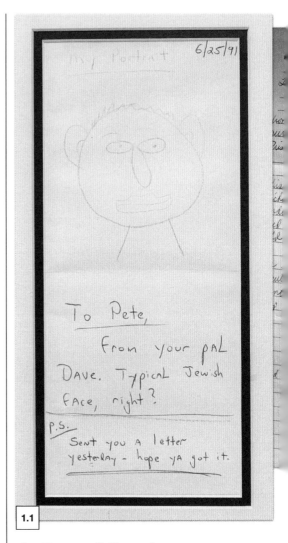

1.1

1. Son of Sam's Self-portrait

David Richard Berkowitz, otherwise known as the Son of Sam or the .44 Caliber Killer, terrorized New York City from July 1976 through July 1977: the Summer(s) of Sam. Not long after Berkowitz was taken into custody by the NYPD in front of his Yonkers apartment building on August 10, 1977, he confessed to the six murders. However, he claimed to be only obeying the orders of a 6000-year-old demon, manifested in the form of a dog belonging to his neighbor, Sam.

1.1 A childlike self-portrait from Berkowitz to a pen pal, suggesting he sees himself as a much less complicated person than he was when he committed his crimes.

Concern,

hair attached hereon was shaved-
serial sex killer Ted Bundy
execution at the Florida State
on January 24, 1989.

is provided to   Sealed as
with the firm   authentic relic
will not be
rials and not
the market.

from the
Bundy
Death

Schaefer — 039506

legal assistant —

2.1

TO: RICHARD DICKSTEIN

The attached paint chip was removed from the FSP death
cell where serial sex killer TED BUNDY spent his
final hours before being shaved, orally tampered and
diapered before being led to his execution by
ELECTROCUTION while strapped to the prison death chair
known throughout the world as "OLD SPARKY".

This paint chip is presented to RICHARD DICKSTEIN by
G.J. SCHAEFER, known in true crime circles as "THE HANGMAN",
and regarded by author ROBERT RESSLER as America's most
accomplished serial killer and TED BUNDY'S closest friend.

This paint chip is presented to RICHARD DICKSTEIN on the SIXTH
ANNIVERSARY of TED BUNDY'S execution carried out on January
24, 1989 by Florida's first female executioner.

PAINT CHIP FROM
DEATH CELL: Q1E1

G.J. Schaefer:
Ted Bundy's friend and legal assistant

2.2

DC3-008

---

2. Not to be Used in Satanic Rituals

Ted Bundy was a monster and a master of multiplicity. His good looks, charisma, and above-average IQ allowed him to win victims' trust before he raped, strangled, and dismembered them. Bundy was convicted of raping and murdering 14 young women; however, he later claimed the number was closer to 30. He was executed via the electric chair on January 24, 1989.

Both of these unique items were obtained via Gerard John Schaefer Jr., an American murderer, suspected serial killer, and fellow death row inmate. The document on the left states that the hair "was shaved from the body of serial sex killer, Ted Bundy, prior to his execution," and is "provided with the firm understanding that it will not be used in satanic rituals." Both documents are signed by Gerard Schaefer, "Ted Bundy's former legal assistant."

2.1 Although there may be a few other examples of Bundy's hair in private collections, this scarce specimen comes from Bundy's body being shaved before execution.

2.2 A paint chip from the wall of Bundy's death row cell. The accompanying document states that it is presented "on the sixth anniversary of Ted Bundy's execution carried out on January 24, 1989 by Florida's first female executioner."

Dr. David R. Adamovich and Lynn J. Wheat

page two

I see this ribbon is going so this will be the la
by the way if you notice that some keys are light
because I had a stroke in '84 and it effect the v
arm hand and eye. Lucky for me the hand still
up and down at night. if you know what I mean?
The games are hard to do in letter but if your i
exchange them either in cartoon xerox's or writi
Like do you know what a condom and Kodak process
ans: They both capture the moment.
You know the defination of a Lesbian? Just anoth
man's job.
What's the object of a Jewish football game? an
Just one more as I don't want you rolling on th
Did you hear about the deck of Rodney King play
comes with one spade and 51 clubs.
                        well my friend I'll lea
                                stay well b

John Gacy N00921
Lock Box 711
Menard, Illinois 62259

Richard H. Dick

Yonkers, N.Y.

John Wayne Gacy N00921   Execute Justice... Not Peopl

Lock Box 711   Richard Dickstein
Menard Illinois
USA 62259   New York 1071
                                 November 7th, 1993

HI HO Richie,
    Tahnks for thelstter and the photos along with the money order for
I appreciate your thinking of me.
    So how is big Richie taking care of Lil' Richie, just remember to
up with your exercise of head over head, as thats a tasty way to sta
in shape. haha.
    Regarding the mail hell in all the years I have been writing I can neve
tell how its going to go out. But anything I do on a fir, sat, or sun
doesn't go out until Monday morning so thats the delay at this end.
as for it taking all the rest of the time well that has to be the post
office service.
    Thanks for the two photo of the Carter deal that was from back in May,'78
when I was in charge of the reception for Mrs Carter. the man off to the
side is Jake Sullivan from secret service. I trust that you didn't get
taken on those photos as they can be found in several books out on me so
this guy didn't have the originals as the one that took the photo was a
White House press man, as my original copy that I had was from the White
House. You asked if I look thrilled, not really since I was incharge and
just a few week later I was with her husband, they are just people with
positions. See my point, just like I tell you that there is nobody better
then you as long as you know your no better then anyone else.
    So how is the new job working out? It ounds like something you could have
fun at while also meeting some new people. You never did say the name of
the dance club was? is it well known? Many known people go there, are
they the yuppie crowd?
    The pay doesn't sound bad for the hours. now all you need to do is find
another one with that kind of pay for that many hours and you would have
it made. good income and low hours.
    Regarding Pres. Clinton Hey I am for the guy and I hope the people give
him a chance to make changes, hell it took Reagan and Bush 12 years to fuck
this cou try up and people expect Clinton to change it back in one year.
It aint going to happen right?
    Yes I know who Joey Buttafuoco is, a total asshole, had he stayed out of
the spot light he would not being having his trouble now.

CONTAINS
OVER 300
"HOW TO
PHOTOS!

3.1

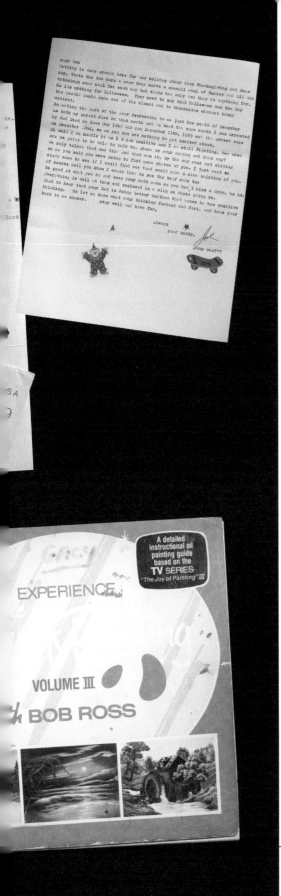

3. The Four Johns

After Manson, John Wayne Gacy is probably the next most recognizable figure in the rogues' gallery of serial killers. So how does a person rape, torture, and kill 33 people, and bury 26 of them in a crawl space under his house and still go undetected?

Gacy had built a reputation as a good neighbor, an enterprising businessman who employed local youth, and an active member of community organizations. However, in late 1978, Gacy surmised that his murderous deeds were about to be found out, and on December 22, he went to the police station to confess. Not long into the confession, Gacy waived his Miranda rights and told detectives, "There are four Johns." He explained there was John the contractor, John the clown, and John the politician. The fourth "John" was Jack Hanley, and it was Jack who was the killer and did all the evil things. We can assume it was Jack Hanley who also joked during his trial, saying the only thing he was guilty of was "running a cemetery without a license."

Gacy was executed by lethal injection in Illinois on May 10, 1994. His final spoken words were reported to be "Kiss my ass."

3.1 A Christmas card with a lock of Gacy's hair and the Bob Ross book (signed by Gacy) reflect the personalities of the three "Johns," whereas the letters display elements of Hanley. They read like a pedophile grooming a potential victim, and include childish stickers of clowns. In one he writes: "I am willing to answer anything as long as the person is just as honest and open with me."

'The fourth "John" was Jack Hanley, and it was Jack who was the killer and did all the evil things.'

The wanted poster on the right depicts the Zodiac from early eyewitnesses.

ABOVE IS A SKETCH OF AN INDIVIDUAL WHO, PRIOR TO THE SHOOTING OF A VICTIM IN CENTRAL PARK ON JUNE 21, 1990, APPROACHED THE VICTIM AND INQUIRED AS TO HIS BIRTHDATE. THE VICTIM WAS SHOT BY THE PERSON DESCRIBED AS THE "ZODIAC GUNMAN."

DESCRIPTION

MALE, BLACK, 33 YEARS OLD, 184 POUNDS. DARK COMPLEXION, BLACK AFRO STYLE HAIR, SLIGHTLY RECEDING OR SLIGHT-BALD SPOT IN FRONT. MUSTACHE, THREE DAY GROWTH OF BEARD. THE INDIVIDUAL WAS WEARING A BLACK NYLON SHORT SLEEVE SHIRT, LEE PRE-WASHED JEANS AND SNEAKERS. HE WORE A BLACK BRACELET ON HIS LEFT WRIST.

POLICE HOTLINE TELEPHONE NUMBER

718-875-0523

4. Copycat Zodiac Killer

Heriberto Seda was a bible-quoting media hound who gave two reasons for killing his victims: first, "they were bad. They were evil people," while the other was to do with their zodiac sign. He was a cut-rate, poor man's Zodiac killer, who terrorized New York City with two short but deadly shooting sprees between 1990 and 1993 that left three dead and five wounded. In this letter to a friend he writes: "By now you will have heard I have been sentenced to about 85 to life. I was shock [sic] by the sentence, I'm doing better now."

4.1 The wanted poster on the right depicts the Zodiac from early eyewitnesses. The newspaper above clearly illustrates why you can never trust eyewitnesses. Or was it the by-product of a highly racially divided New York City of the early 1990s?

5. A Killer's Killer

Christopher Scarver's infamy was not established by how many people he killed (although he did murder three), but rather by who he killed. Diagnosed as a schizophrenic psychopath with messianic delusions, Scarver was serving a sentence for two counts of first-degree murder when, on November 28, 1994, he was teamed with two other inmates to clean the prison bathroom. Under the suspicious circumstances of being left without guard watch in the bathroom, Scarver beat his fellow inmates to death with a metal pipe. One of the murdered inmates was the infamous cannibal Jeffrey Dahmer. Scarver said that Dahmer had taunted him as well as other inmates by constructing "severed limbs" out of food and ketchup.

5.1 In this letter, Scarver's delusional thoughts are quickly cut short by a skirmish between a guard and an inmate happening two cells away.

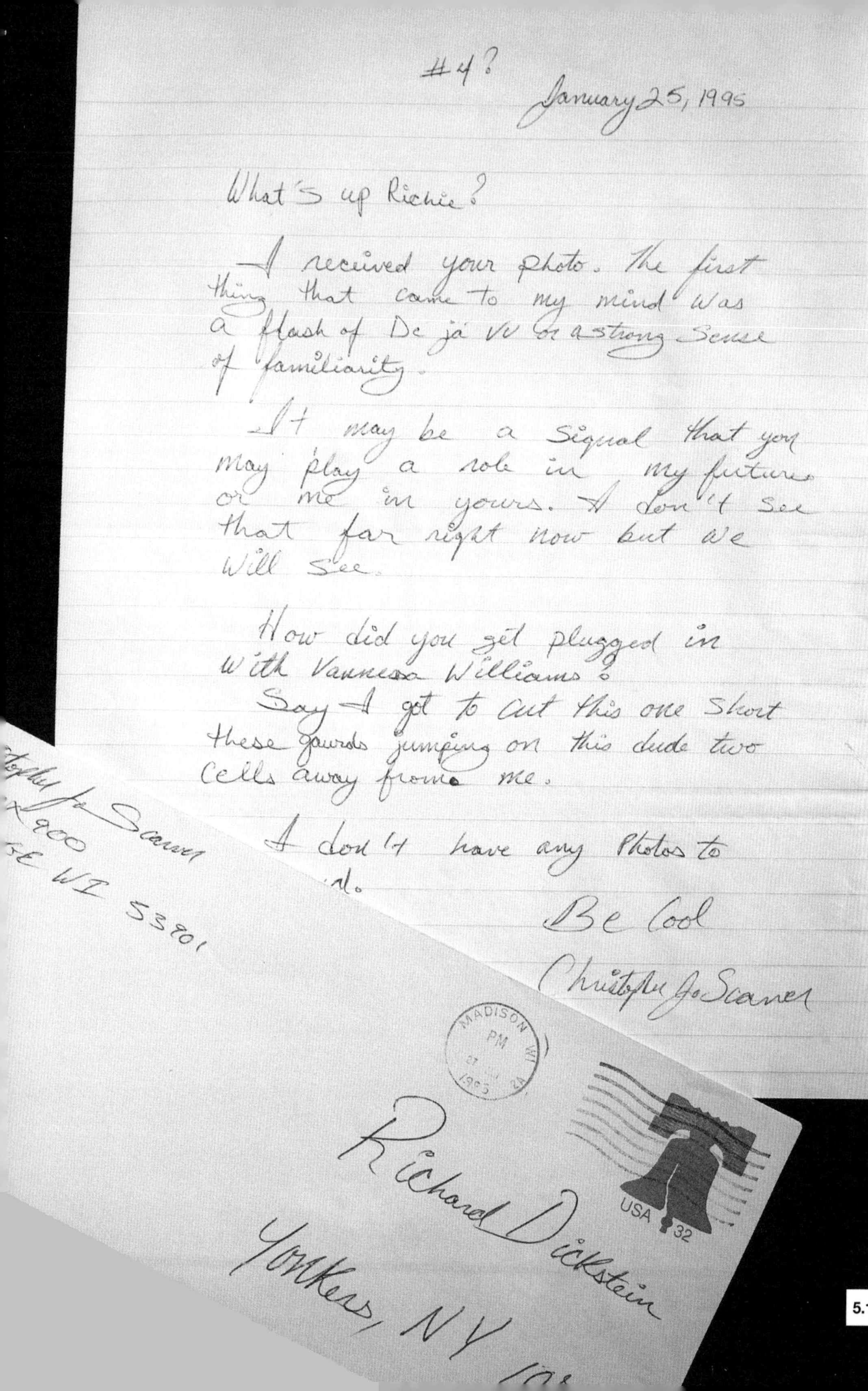

#4?

January 25, 1995

What's up Richie?

I received your photo. The first thing that came to my mind was a flash of Deja vu or a strong sense of familiarity.

It may be a signal that you may play a role in my future or me in yours. I don't see that far right now but we will see.

How did you get plugged in with Vanessa Williams?

Say I got to cut this one short these gaurds jumping on this dude two cells away from me.

I don't have any photos to ...d.

Be Cool

Christopher Jo Scaner

MADISON
PM
WI
1995
Richard Dickstein
Yonkers, NY
USA
32

5.1

6.1

Robert,
9/11/94

Feel weird writing to my own name. If you know what I mean! Thanx for the 25 and pictures. Greatly appreciated. I used to go to Downtown LA to take pictures like that. There was a place where I could go under the streets. It was at a stop light. I'd be able to look up the cunts dresses as they would wait for the walk sign to change. I'd take pictures. You'd be suprised at how many chicks walk around w/ no panties. Swimming pools + beaches are excellent places too. I got a catologue that sells all kinds of different high pumps + stuff. Let me know if you want the address. Well, here it is just in case you want it: Photrix Box 431 Hollywood CA 90078. They got a lot of good shit. So it took almost 24 days for you to get my letter huh? Fucking figures. These fuckers like to fuck up my mail. That's why they're called fuckers. I'll send the photo soon. Did you get the MTV awards Sean Penn at LA cou in jail for 30 days a camera man. She ca and I saw her. She's

something about Hollywood chicks that I dig. Her calves and ankles are definitely healthy. I think you'd agree. Man you saw that movie Ben Kelly. They gets me pictures in it. So whadja think of that airplane that went down? Still, I'm sure there were a few severed feet still in their pumps out there. ha ha. Am I sick or what? And proud of it.

Till we meet again
The Beast from the East

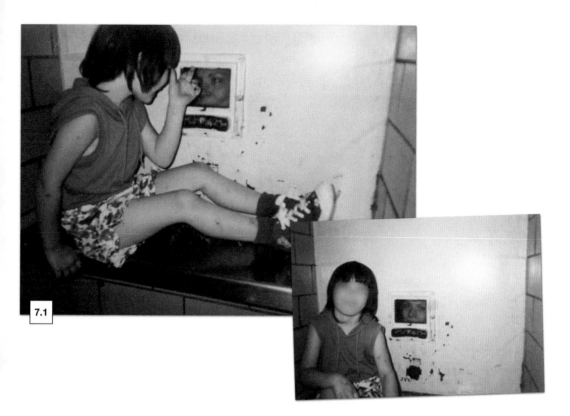

7.1

6. Ramirez the Reaper

Richard "the Night Stalker" Ramirez was obsessed with deviant sex and claimed to be prompted by Satan to carry out his rapes and murders. Compared to many other notorious serial killers, he committed his crimes over a relatively short two years. However, within those 24 months, he was prolific. In 1989, the 29-year-old Ramirez was sentenced to death for the conviction of 13 murders, 5 attempted murders, 11 sexual assaults, and 14 burglaries. His courtroom response to the sentence was, "Big deal. Death always went with the territory. See you in Disneyland." Ramirez spent 23 years on death row before succumbing to B-cell lymphoma in 2013.

6.1 **This letter is a testament to Ramirez's lack of remorse and continued obsession with sex. In it he also mentions seeing Madonna while he awaited trial in LA County Jail. She had been visiting Sean Penn, when he was serving time for parole violation in 1987. Ramirez's drawing shows a reaper, a favorite subject of his, but this is a rare full-body reaper with a sickle.**

7. High-Security Visit

As a result of a drug- and alcohol-fueled murderous rampage, LaFonda Foster and Tina Powell viciously killed five people in less than 12 hours on the night of April 23–24, 1986. The five victims were reportedly "friends" of Foster and Powell's. The two women shot, stabbed, ran over, and burned their victims alive. In February 1987, a jury found both women guilty on all five counts of first-degree murder. LaFonda Foster was sentenced to death and Tina Powell received a life sentence. In 1991 Foster's death sentence was overturned to life in prison.

7.1 **A sobering image of LaFonda Foster only being able to interact with her young visitor through the thick glass of a tiny window in her high-security visitation cell.**

The note in image 8.1 reads:

I recently began shaving my head every week again, but used the clippers to save some locks for those few who've asked. Here is one, from the side of my head. I'm now bald on top.

Roy L. Norris
RIGHT THUMBPRINT
12-1-94

8. Deadly Combination

Roy Lewis Norris was one half of the torture/rape/murder duo known as the Tool Box Killers. Along with Lawrence Bittaker, he preyed on teenage girls from June through October 1979. Before that, Norris had spent five years at Atascadero State Hospital for attacking a young woman on the San Diego State College campus. He tackled the student, bashed her head with a stone, and then slammed her head repeatedly into the cement sidewalk.

He was released on probation and described as a person "who would bring no further danger to others." That proved inaccurate as Norris was eventually convicted of the first- and second-degree murder, kidnapping, and rape of five women. He was sentenced to 45 years to life with the possibility of parole, but died in prison of natural causes in 2020, aged 72.

8.1 For a select few, Norris would send clippings of his hair. This particular specimen also includes his fingerprint.

8.2 A creepy "multi-portrait" by Norris, showing his partner-in-crime Bittaker on the left and himself on the right, the two combining into "Death."

9.1

9. Snippets of Manson

Charles Miles Manson is arguably the most recognizable and written-about serial killer of modern times. His reign of terror officially ended on January 25, 1971, when a jury found Manson, Patricia Krenwinkel, and Susan Atkins guilty of first-degree murder in seven of the Tate–LaBianca killings, and Manson was sentenced to death (commuted to life imprisonment in 1972).

One of the countless macabre aspects of Manson's psychological profile was his some-times childlike approach to serious and deadly situations, in which eruptions of violence would be offset with outbursts of silliness.

9.1 Charles Manson's hair was an iconic aspect of his appearance, whether his long flowing locks, the crew cut of his first incarceration, or the wild styles he created before each parole hearing. The deep black of these curls suggests they were cut off early in his incarceration.

9.2 These two rambling letters and postcard reflect some of the convoluted sociopathic traits that mesmerized so many of Manson's followers. ATWA (an acronym for Air, Trees, Water, Animals and All the Way Alive) is the ecological belief system propounded by Manson. [Over the page.]

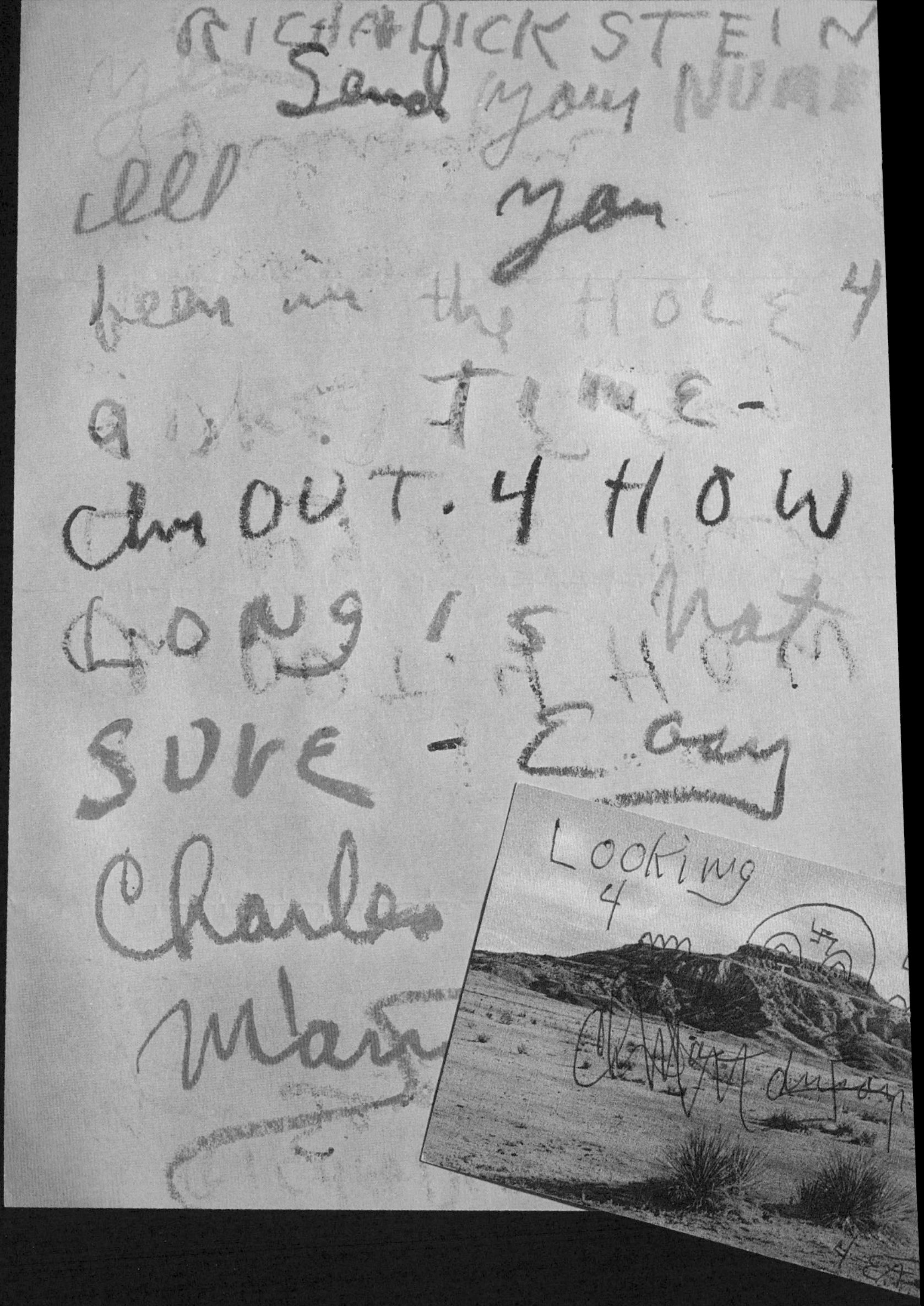

RICHADICKSTEIN

Send your NUMB

ill you

been in the HOLE 4

a big time -

cm OUT. 4 HOW

LONG i s Not

sure - E asy

Charles

Mason

Looking 4

...isket Tasket The Headmans Basket –
How meany has been loped off
...y the golden sword – all will ruin
...en seiver, for the reward but
...lone forever, may be tis tru
with out your love it would
...uch Shapes & forms formed
...hrine – what now ry rose bu
...tattered Shadered Tout Hou
...Matter, word Symbels
...to whos who un Cou
...iif thats all thats real
...at by the battel fields + past
...befor me mine farnel if me suy
...mere – Charl<u>Yae</u> M <u>Bussup</u>
:ATWA: ps JUST WORDS
af WOT

TAKEN AT CORCORAN
STATE PRISON, CALIFERNIA
MARCH – 1999.

History of Lena & Ashley
Ordeal

Feb-6-1961 - Crime Comitted
Feb-28-1961 - Arrested in New York
March 5-1961- brought back to Houston
May 15-1961- first Trial
May 29-1961- got death sentence
Feb 31 -1963 - first date
March 30 1963 - Governor 30 day stay
March 30-1963 - 4 hours from death
    Judge Brown granted New Hearing
April 9. 1963
April 9, 1963 - Gov Connally gave
    stay till May 31.
In New Orleans - May 9. Appeal for
New trial was heard by 3 Judges
    June 26, 1963 - got New trial

10.1

10.1

11.1

10. The Beatnik Killers

On the night of February 6, 1961, Carolyn Lima and her transgender friend Leslie Douglas Ashley arrived at the office of Fred Tones for a prearranged, paid sexual encounter. Something went wrong, and Tones was shot six times and his lifeless body set ablaze. Lima and Ashley were on the run for three weeks before the FBI captured them. The "Beatnik Killers"—as the Houston Press referred to them—faced charges of capital murder. They had a joint trial, at which both claimed to have killed Tones in self-defense. On May 24, 1961, an all-male Harris County jury passed a guilty verdict and sentenced both to death. Lima and Ashley sat on death row for almost two years before being issued stays of execution just hours before they were scheduled to die. On conclusion of their second trials, Lima was sentenced to five years in prison, while Ashley was declared insane and sent to a San Antonio psychiatric hospital. Ashley eventually had gender confirmation surgery.

10.1 Although it cannot be verified, based on the Western Union Telegram these documents and photos appear to have been the property of Carolyn Lima's mother.

The notebook page lists the "History of Lima and Ashley's Ordeal." How heartbreaking to receive the notice of your child's impending execution via a telegram. To add insult to injury, there is a critical typo, reading "said" in the place of "sad."

11. Suicide Bunk Bed

On March 26, 1997, authorities entered "The Monastery," a mansion rented by the Heaven's Gate religious cult near San Diego. They found the bodies of 39 people, who had committed mass suicide by taking a cocktail of barbiturates and vodka. The deceased all wore matching sweatsuits and Nike sneakers. In their pockets, they each had a five-dollar bill and three quarters, apparently in homage to a version of the book *The Adventures of Huckleberry Finn*, which states that it costs five dollars and seventy-five cents to ride the tail of a comet to heaven. The 39 bodies lay neatly on the bunk beds, their belief having been that post-mortem they'd soon be transported by spaceship to a new beginning.

11.1 One of the Heaven's Gate bunk beds, acquired initially through an estate sale auction in 1999.

Dr. David R. Adamovich and Lynn J. Wheat

175

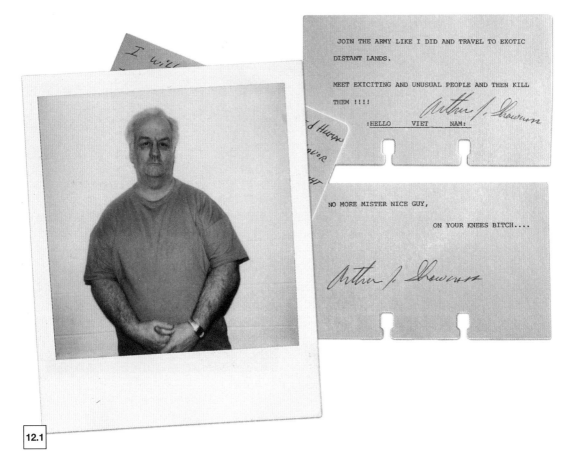

JOIN THE ARMY LIKE I DID AND TRAVEL TO EXOTIC
DISTANT LANDS.

MEET EXICITING AND UNUSUAL PEOPLE AND THEN KILL
THEM !!!!

:HELLO   VIET   NAM:

NO MORE MISTER NICE GUY,

ON YOUR KNEES BITCH....

12.1

12. The Genesee River Killer

Arthur Shawcross, "the Genesee River Killer," had a low IQ of 86. A troubled man (he claimed his mother abused him, his aunt performed oral sex on him when he was nine, and that he had incestuous relations with his sister during junior high school), he was also a bed-wetter and spoke in "baby talk" up to the age of six.

In May 1972, Shawcross raped and killed a ten-year-old boy (his first known victim) after luring the boy into the woods outside of Watertown, New York. Three months later, he raped and killed an eight-year-old girl. Shawcross was arrested the following day. He spent 14 years at Green Haven Correctional Facility, and was released on parole in April 1987 when social workers had concluded that Shawcross was "no longer dangerous." This disregarded the warnings of psychiatrists, who had assessed Shawcross as a "schizoid psychopath."

From March 1988 through December 1989, Shawcross raped and violently murdered at least 11 women, most of whom were found near the Genesee River. He was sentenced to 250 years in 1991 and died in prison of a heart attack on November 10, 2008.

12.1 A Polaroid of Shawcross taken in prison. These Rolodex cards are a prime example of Shawcross's sick sense of humor, revealing that he had no sympathy, empathy, or remorse for his heinous acts.

'Social workers had concluded that Shawcross was "no longer dangerous."'

"When a woman insists on being an ass, it's only polite to ride her as far as she wants to go"

Arthur J. Shawcross
Feb 1988

WHEN I DIE, I HOPE THEY BURY ME UPSIDE DOWN....

SO THE WHOLE WORLD CAN KISS ME FUCKING ASS!!!!

Arthur J. Shawcross

:S T R E S S:

THAT CONFUSION CREATED WHEN ONE'S MIND OVERRIDES THE
BODY'S BASIC DESIRE TO CHOKE THE LIVING SHIT OUT OF
SOME ASSHOLE WHO DESPERATELY NEEDS IT!!!!

Arthur J. Shawcross

:S T R E S S:

THAT CONFUSION CREATED WHEN ONE'S MIND OVERRIDES THE BODYS
BASIC DESIRE TO CHOKE THE LIVING SHIT OUT OF SOME ASS-
HOLE WHO DESPERATELY NEEDS IT!!!!

Arthur J. Shawcross

You know of what
I mean....HAHA!

"LADIES"

IF YOU ARE LOOKING FOR THAT MOST UNUSUAL SENSATION IN
LIFE, I WOULD ADVISE YOU TO CONTACT ME AS SOON AS YOU
CAN GET YOUR ADDRESS IN THE MAIL!!!!
COME UP FOR A VISIT, DON'T WARE ANY UNDERPANTS.....

Arthur J. Shawcross

IF YOU ARE ONE OF THE ON THE GO PEOPLE AND LIKE TO

TRAVEL, GO ON HIKES, THEN TAKE A FUCKING WALK IN THE

WOODS WITH ME!!!!

Arthur J. Shawcross

I HAVE NOT HAD SEX IN SO LONG THAT I FORGOT WHO IT

WAS THAT GET'S TIED UP, YOU OF THE GIRL IN THE OTHER

ROOM!!!!!

Arthur J. Shawcross

13. Still Manson's Girl

Lynette Alice "Squeaky" Fromme is infamous for her "quality time" spent with the Manson Family and her public displays of affection for Charles Manson. However, she was cleared of any involvement with the Tate–LaBianca murders. The 34 years she served of a life sentence were for her assassination attempt on U.S. President Gerald Ford in 1975.

Fromme was released on parole from Federal Medical Center, Carswell, on August 14, 2009. In a TV interview ten years later, she was asked about her feelings for Charles Manson; she replied, "Was I in love with Charlie? Yeah, oh yeah. I still am." She added, "I feel very honored to have met him, and I know how that sounds to people who think he's the epitome of evil."

In this letter to a pen pal in 1996, Fromme writes, "I am not good for you. I would hurt your feelings. You want to know about EVIL and I'd say good luck. Everybody's looking for something," and signs off by writing "ATWA", the acronym coined by Charles Manson (see page 171).

13.1 In this letter, written on the backs of three postcards, Fromme is suspicious of her pen pal and implies there may be ulterior motives behind the correspondence. She responds to previous questions by asking, "Do you really want to know, or are you looking for something to sell?"

'You want to know about EVIL and I'd say good luck. Everybody's looking for something.'

The ruby-throated hummingbird (*Archilochus colubris*). Copyright © 1985 Robert A. Tyrrell.

From Tyrrell, *Hummingbirds Photo Postcards*, a Dover pub

13.1

Barbara Nista
820
Scars...

think of this world we are living in. I wonder what world you are living in. You don't seem to have an opinion of your own or a real feeling — even though whatever it is is real to you. People are frequently different in writing than in person you wouldn't like calling you an air head or any other label and I wouldn't like it either. I would rather you had your experiences and learned and

3) grew + were thrown + fell + maybe got up + understood you because that's all you or anyone really has. Quote "Friendship is something that I hold dear to my heart, not that you care, but this is just how I feel. Did you ever have a friend that you felt this way about?" That ... by Charlie White. Who are you asking for? I've been in prison 2... years Do you really want to know or are you looking for something to sell. I am not good for you. I would hurt your feelings. You want to know about EVIL and I'd say good luck. Everybody's looking for something. Good luck you want to know about survival — ATWA. Lynette

Published by SCOPE ENTERPRISES, P.O. Box 85, Clovis, CA 93

GENERAL LEE TREE
KINGS CANYON NATIONAL PARK, CALIFORNIA
This giant sequoia is located in the Grant Grove. It is 254 feet high and 22 feet in diameter. In the background is the Fallen Monarch, a fire-hollowed log so huge that the opening was used by the 4th U.S. Cavalry as a stable for their horses in bad weather.
SE-698

PHOTOGRAPH BY ARNOLD AND CAROLE COMPOMONGO

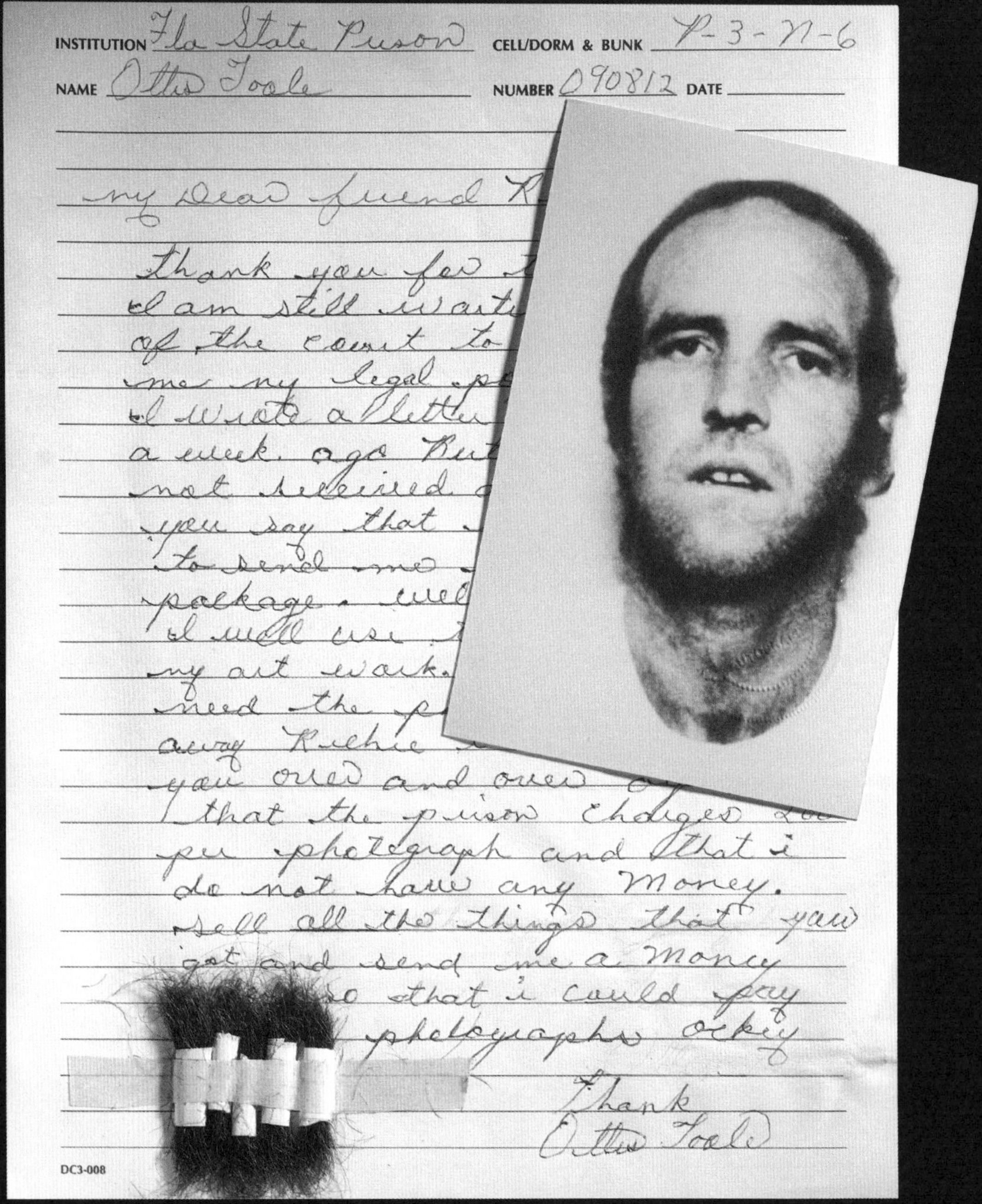

INSTITUTION *Fla State Prison* CELL/DORM & BUNK *P-3-N-6*

NAME *Ottis Toole* NUMBER *090812* DATE _____

My Dear friend R_____

Thank you for _____
I am still waiti_____
of the court to _____
me my legal pe_____
I wrote a letter _____
a week ago But _____
not recieved _____
you say that _____
to send me _____
package. well _____
I will use _____
my art work. _____
need the p_____
away Richie _____
you owed and over _____
that the prison charges _____
per photograph and that i
do not have any money.
sell all the things that you
got and send me a money
_____ so that i could pay
_____ photographs okey

Thank

Ottis Toole

DC3-008

5.25.mn

Dearest Barbara:

I'm stunned. They forwarded your letter to me a few days ago and I was literally stunned wordless. I still am. Wow! You must feel devastated. I feel so bad for you. I realize how very special Muffin was and still is to you. Seventeen wonderful years that also illustrates how good a care giver you were to her. Muffin was very lucky that you and she came together. You gave her a wonderful life always remember that. You gave each other love. Always remember that love and joy that you gave to each other. That is what is most special and what is the most important.

The pain and loss that you feel now will fade thats one of the special things about time. But good memories last a lifetime. One thing that I am happy about is that I was able to do that painting for you. You will never forget her and that painting will always help to keep the memories bright.

I wish you heart peace

Sincerely with all my love

Joel

14. Toole the Ghoul

It feels like no coincidence that Toole rhymes with ghoul, though some say fate dealt Ottis Elwood Toole a cruel hand, leading to his demonic behavior. Toole's alcoholic father abandoned the family early on, and according to Toole his abusive mother dressed him as a girl. He also claimed that, as a child, he was the victim of sexual assaults and incest at the hands of relatives and family friends, including his older sister and a neighbor. He maintained that his grandmother was a satanist and exposed him in childhood to satanic practices and rituals, including self-mutilation and grave robbing, and nicknamed him the "Devil's Child." In addition, Toole had an IQ of 75.

Toole later teamed up with psychopath Henry Lee Lucas, and from 1976 through 1983, claimed to have raped and killed between six and 65 people. Although authorities can only confirm six of the claims, one verified victim is six-year-old Adam Walsh. Toole decapitated Walsh with a machete and then drove around for several days with the boy's head. Eventually, he forgot about it, and when he found it, threw it into a canal.

Adam's murder prompted his father, John Walsh, to create the popular show *America's Most Wanted*.

14.1 Letter and photograph sent from Ottis Toole to a correspondent. He taped four small bunches of his hair to the letter in neatly packed rolls.

15. The Killer Cat Lover

Mainly preying on sex workers, Joel David Rifkin went on a killing spree from 1989 through 1993. He was arrested after a routine traffic stop revealed the decomposing body of 22-year-old Tiffany Brescian wrapped in plastic in the back of his pickup truck. In 1994, Rifkin was ultimately found guilty of nine murders and suspected of eight more. He was sentenced to 203 years to life.

15.1 A letter from Rifkin to a pen pal, in which he comforts her on the death of her cat, Muffin, saying, "The pain and loss that you feel now will fade, that's one of the special things about time." Clearly having more regard for felines than humans, also shown here is a careful drawing Rifkin did of a cat named Samantha.

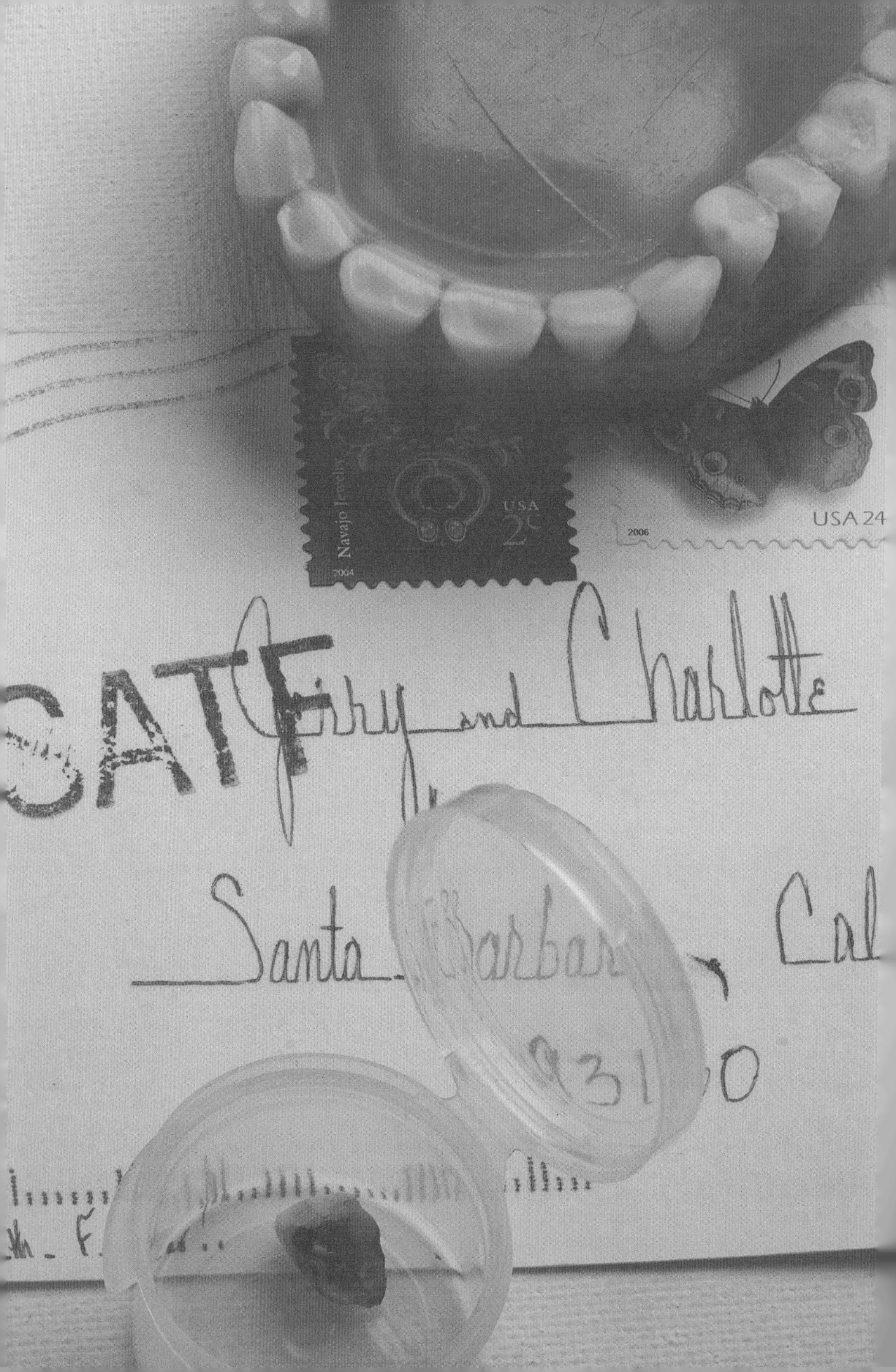

GATE Firby and Charlotte

Santa Barbara, Cal

931 0

A FAUSTIAN BARGAIN

"Hello, this is a collect call from an inmate at the California State Prison, Sacramento. To accept the charges ..." The general public would be shocked to discover how easy it is to reach out to high-profile inmates. There are websites devoted to publishing the names and addresses of thousands of people who are incarcerated, some for life or even on death row. On average, Charles Manson received hundreds of letters a week. John Wayne Gacy was sent so many requests for friendship that he responded with a questionnaire that the potential pen pal would have to fill out and return before he would even consider starting up a relationship.

The phenomenon of women writing to inmates is partially fueled by the men behind bars knowing just what to say in their letters. According to an anonymous female correction officer, the inmates use one of four tactics: "You're not like other women"; "You're so beautiful/sexy/hot"; "You make me want to be a better person"; or "You can do better than me".

William Harder's collection is an example of inmate correspondence going beyond "pen-pal status." A portrait of himself and his wife with their arms around Lawrence Bittaker and Roy Norris, painted by serial killer Fernando Caro, is a perfect case in point of how personal some of the collector's relationships with inmates have become. "Which is why, when asked if I have a prized possession, I have to respond that my prized possession isn't a tangible thing, it's the collective experience—my life with the thrill kill cult. For example, nothing I own can replace the real-life, in-person interactions I've had with Charles Manson."

When it comes to morality and the concept of collecting, William believes it's all subjective: "I don't wear fur or leather, but you don't see me going around giving my two cents to folks who do." However, he is quick to clarify that when it comes to his website, Murder Auction, he has rules regarding a few items that he feels cross the line. Although, despite the limitations he does enforce, "Victim types still curse my name; most offenders still feel it's a disgusting practice, but collectors still want these items."

The collection of G. William Harder

William Harder's route into the world of true crime collecting had an innocent inception. As a child living in Spain, he began collecting sharks' teeth then the more conventional baseball cards. It all changed in 2000, when he wrote to his first serial killer and received a response: a letter addressed to Mr. William Harder with a return address from Richard "the Night Stalker" Ramirez via San Quentin State Prison.

William can't say for sure why that initial Ramirez response started the ball rolling. "Why does a person collect anything? I also collect travel spoons and coins, Spanish mud people, human bones, and Judeo-Christian-related items, mainly crucifixes. The collecting of Christian artifacts sort of falls into the true crime theme for me. I believe organized religions have been a scourge on humanity, leaving an ever-growing pile of bodies in their wake."

William had a few brushes with the law as a youth, most of them substance-related, and he found himself in the custody of the State of California at the age of 20. "I ended up forfeiting two years of my life for those actions. But it's the way life goes sometimes. I don't identify as a victim. Since that incarceration, I've visited over 90 convicted murderers. And I am in contact with many, many inmates almost daily."

Photos by Dan Howell

1.1

1. My Wife, by the Tourniquet Killer

Anthony Shore was an American serial killer and child molester convicted of killing one woman and three girls between 1986 and 2000. He was deemed the "Tourniquet Killer" in response to his use of a ligature to kill his victims. Shore was sentenced to death in 2004 and executed by lethal injection on January 18, 2018.

1.1 A pencil portrait of the collector's wife, Charlotte, based on a photograph given to Shore by the collector. Shore commented that the most challenging section of the picture was drawing the inverted pentagram necklace.

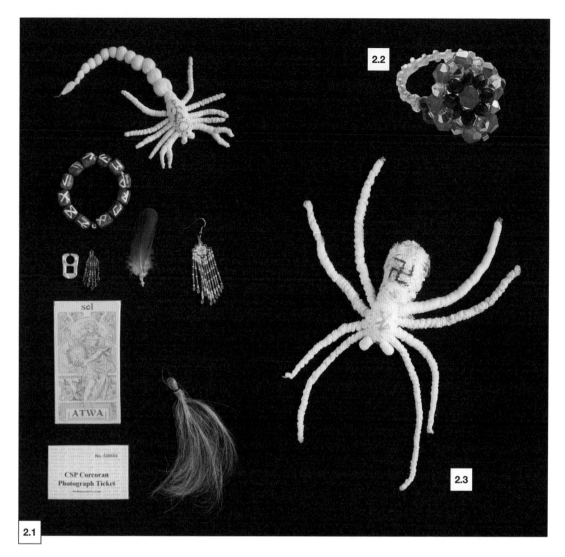

2. Manson Mementos

William Harder maintained a personal relationship with the mastermind behind the Tate–LaBianca murders up until Manson's death in 2017. As well as corresponding with the notorious killer-cult leader, the collector visited Manson on numerous occasions, declaring, "I took more from my interactions with Manson than any other inmate. He had a wisdom about him that was life-changing."

2.1 Scorpion string art and beaded bracelet made of toilet paper. "The soda tab was from one of our visits. Manson preferred Mountain Dew, Pepsi, and A&W Root beer. The glass beaded items and feathers were things he gave to me. The ATWA tarot card is signed by Manson. There's a healthy lock of Manson's hair. And a Corcoran prison photo ducat, which is required to take pictures during visits."

2.2 This beaded ring was made by Manson Family member and convicted murderer Susan Atkins. According to the collector, Susan "made this ring for my wife, which she wore during our wedding. We needed 'something blue' and this was just perfect!"

2.3 String art spider bearing a swastika, created by Manson. "This spider was my first string art, a gift from Manson and Star." (Star was Manson's fiancée when he was incarcerated.)

2.4

2.5

2.4 Los Angeles County booking and release documents from October 29 and 30, 1968. This is before the Tate–LaBianca murders were planned.

2.5 Original courtroom sketch of Manson during the trial.

2.6 Polaroid photos taken during some of the collector's visits with Manson.

'I took more from my interactions with Manson than any other inmate. He had a wisdom about him that was life-changing.'

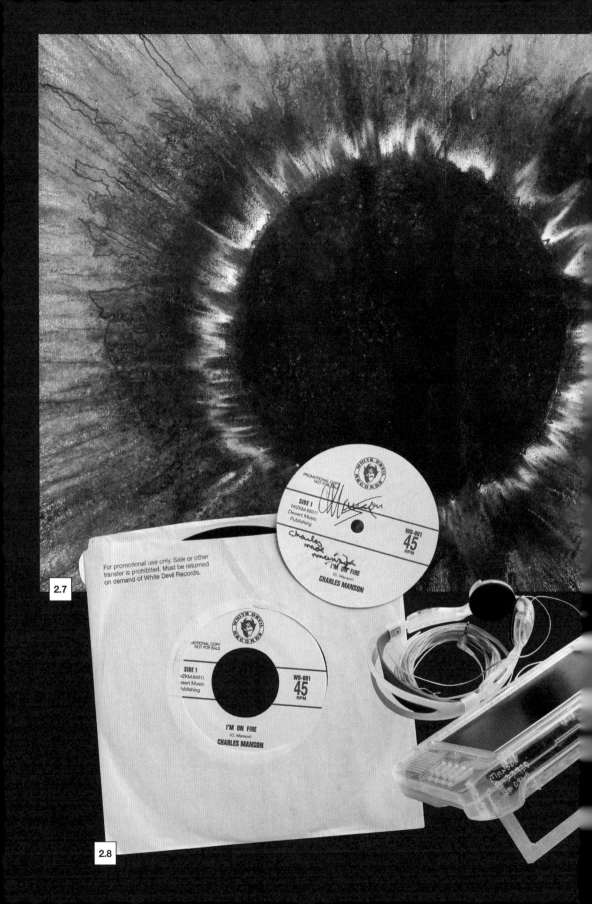

2.7

2.8

2.7 Original Manson artwork showing a black sun. "Manson went outside, looked into the sun, and attempted to put what he saw down on paper."

2.8 A copy of the 45 rpm record of Charles Manson's "I'm On Fire" backed with "The Hallways of the Always," one of the many recordings Manson made while in prison via tape recorders in the 1980s, and a twice-signed label. "Someone tracked down an unused 45 label and mailed it to Manson, who in turn mailed it to me."

2.9 Television and headphones used by Manson while in Corcoran State Prison.

'Manson went outside, looked into the sun, and attempted to put what he saw down on paper.'

2.9

3. The Demon Art of The Night Stalker

Upon being convicted of 13 counts of murder, five counts of attempted murder, and 11 counts of sexual assault, Richard "the Night Stalker" Ramirez eventually received 19 death sentences for his crimes. He was serving time on San Quentin's death row when William Harder struck up a pen-pal correspondence with him, also visiting the killer on several occasions, until Ramirez's death in 2013.

3.1 This is one of the collector's favorite letters from Ramirez: "In it, he remarks that he can't keep up with all the girlfriends I have and signs off with 'Your friend 666.'" Ramirez also answers a question about his foot fetish, saying, "Chix feet? Hell if I know. It's a fetish. From the time I was 9. There's mags devoted to it and Ted Bundy and Pisces people are into em."

3.2 Doreen Ramirez (née Lioy, who had begun writing to Ramirez in 1985 and married him in 1996) eventually ended the relationship and elected to sell off everything of his. This was one of those items, a shirt he had worn in court during the trial.

3.3 "This was the first drawing Ramirez ever sent to me," says William. Ramirez had famously opened his hand to reveal a Satanic pentagram symbol while in court on trial, so this would appear to be a sinister self-portrait.

3.4 Much of Ramirez's artwork features knives and demonic characters. This painting is a more finessed version of the first sketch Ramirez sent to the collector.

3.5 This demonic jester came from the collection of Tobias Allen, one of the earlier collectors of murder memorabilia. Tragically Allen would take his own life in 2007.

3.6 An unsettling depiction of a devil-like reptilian creature.

3.1

3.2

3.3

3.4

3.5

3.6

4.1

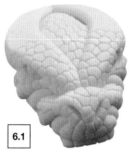

5.1

6.1

4. Yosemite Park Killer's Self-Portrait

Cary Stayner was convicted and sentenced to death for the murders of four women near Yosemite National Park between February and July 1999: a mother, her teenage daughter, the daughter's teenage friend, and Yosemite Institute naturalist Joie Ruth Armstrong. He pleaded not guilty by reason of insanity, his lawyers claiming that the Stayner family had a history of sexual abuse and mental illness. Indeed, Cary's younger brother Steven Stayner was kidnapped at seven years old and did not manage to escape until he was 14.

In return for his confession Cary Stayner asked to be provided with child pornography, a request that was denied. He is still on death row at San Quentin Penitentiary in California.

4.1 | This self-portrait of Stayner was initially submitted to a San Francisco art show. When it was returned, Stayner opted to send it to the collector, who says, "I've kept it ever since. His artwork is something special."

5. The Viper Club

Dennis Rader, the BTK Killer, often refers to memorabilia collectors as "vipers," folks who misrepresent their intentions to get items for collections or resale. William elaborates: "When I first wrote to Dennis, I learned someone had already been in his ear about me. Those lies, mixed with the fact I owned the Murder Auction website, rendered me the King Viper. That woman's attempt at slander failed miserably, and it inspired this piece."

5.1 | Rader, "the woman," and William immortalized in a Rader drawing of "the Viper Club."

6. Soap Carvings

In May 2001, Carl W. Abuhl was convicted of second-degree murder for killing his friend and former roommate Steven Bowen. Before sentencing, Abuhl gave a rambling statement: "Bowen deserved to die for dishonoring my girlfriend and threatening me." In 2004, while at Spring Creek Correctional Center, Abuhl strangled his cellmate, Gregory Beaudoin, to death.

6.1 | Highly detailed dragon and eagle head soap carvings made by Abuhl in prison.

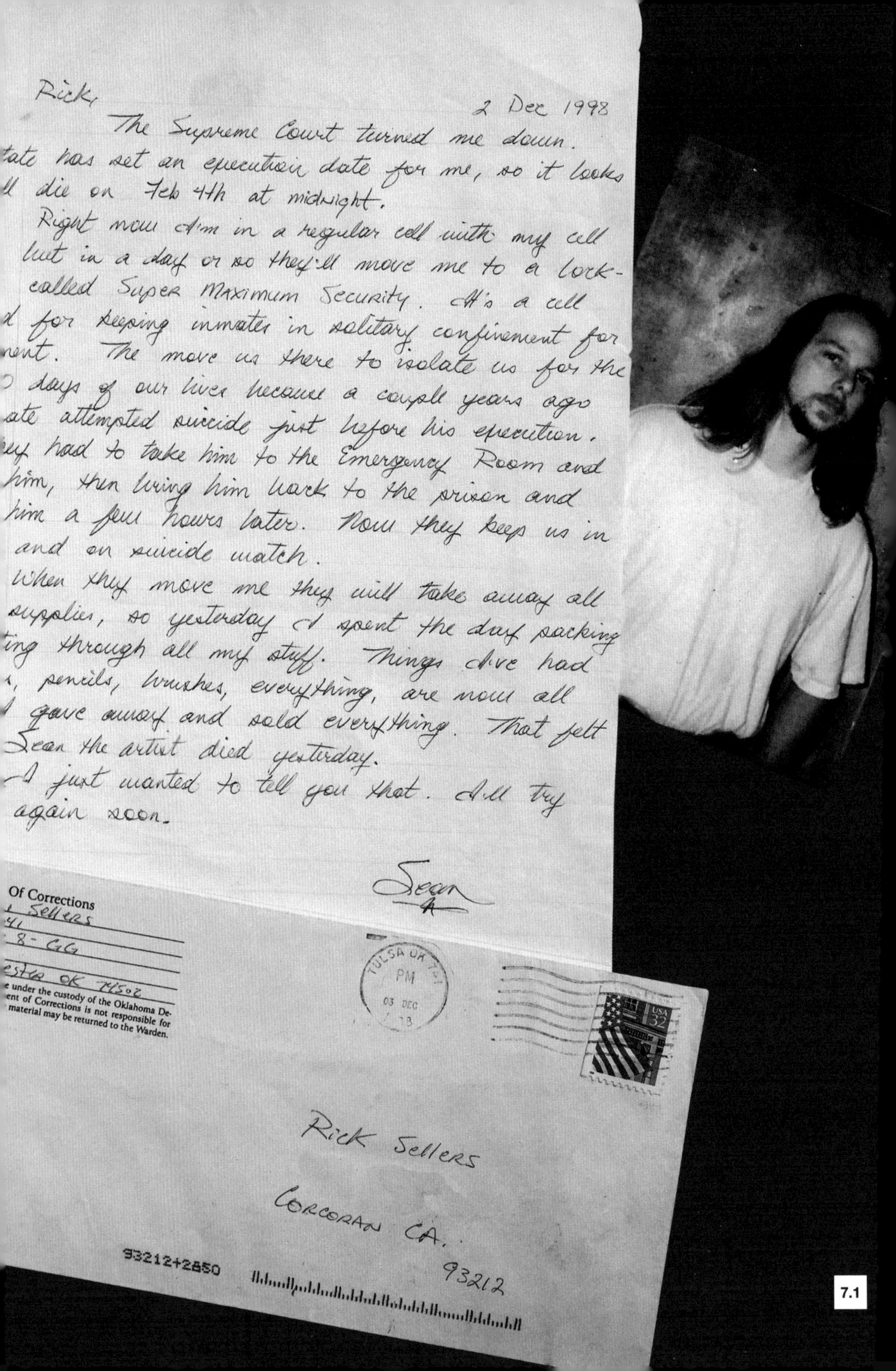

Rick,

2 Dec 1998

The Supreme Court turned me down.
tate has set an execution date for me, so it looks
ll die on Feb 4th at midnight.
Right now I'm in a regular cell with my cell
but in a day or so they'll move me to a lock-
called Super Maximum Security. It's a cell
d for keeping inmates in solitary confinement for
nent. The move us there to isolate us for the
days of our lives because a couple years ago
ate attempted suicide just before his execution.
ey had to take him to the Emergency Room and
him, then bring him back to the prison and
him a few hours later. Now they keep us in
and on suicide watch.
When they move me they will take away all
supplies, so yesterday I spent the day packing
ting through all my stuff. Things I've had
, pencils, brushes, everything, are now all
I gave away and sold everything. That felt
Sean the artist died yesterday.
I just wanted to tell you that. I'll try
again soon.

Sean

Of Corrections
Sellers
41
8-GG
ester OK 74502
e under the custody of the Oklahoma De-
ent of Corrections is not responsible for
material may be returned to the Warden.

TULSA OK 741
PM
03 DEC
98

USA 32

Rick Sellers
Corcoran CA.
93212

93212+2850

7.1

7.2

7. Underage Killer

In March 1985 Sean Sellers was just 16 years old and convicted of murdering his mother, stepfather, and a convenience store clerk. Sellers would blame his murderous actions on demonic possession and converted to Christianity while in prison.

Sellers was one of only 22 people in the United States since the death penalty was reinstated in 1976 to be executed for a crime committed while under the age of 18, and the only person to have been executed for a crime committed while under the age of 17. Sellers was executed on February 4, 1999.

7.1 This letter was given to William by Sean's biological father, Richard Sellers. In it Sean tells his father that the date for his execution has been set and he will be moved to isolation and placed on suicide watch. He also says that he has now given away or sold all of his belongings, including his art supplies: "That felt awful. Sean the artist died yesterday."

7.2 Sean sent this painting to his biological father. There's a small flower in the painting, inside which Sean painted a tiny happy face, an homage to the drawings he used to do with his dad in happier times.

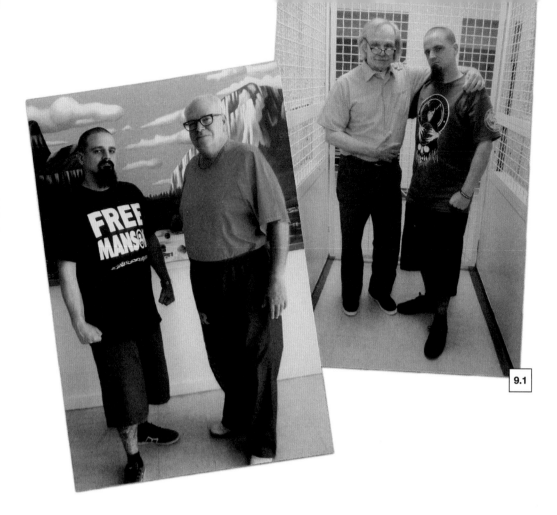

8. All in the Family

In 1980 Fernando Caro was sentenced to death by a Santa Clara County jury, having been found guilty of three counts of first-degree murder and one count of attempted murder. Caro's death sentence was later reduced in 2002 by an appeals court, which found that he did not have adequate legal representation. Caro was found dead in his San Quentin jail cell in 2017. The cause of death was undetermined.

8.1 The collector commissioned Caro to paint a "family" portrait of himself and his wife Charlotte standing with Lawrence Bittaker and Roy Norris: "I picked out clothing from the 1930s. However, there was a miscommunication between Caro and myself, and the prison outfits that were traditionally black stripes with red lettering are all in red. It's still a handsome piece."

9. Blood Brothers

Lawrence Bittaker and Roy Norris kidnapped, raped, tortured, and killed five teenage girls in southern California over five months in 1979. They were "blood brothers," at least until Norris accepted a plea bargain, whereby he agreed to testify against Bittaker in return for receiving life imprisonment with the possibility of parole after serving 30 years. He died of natural causes at the California Medical Facility in February 2020.

9.1 Visitation photos of the collector with Norris at the Substance Abuse Treatment Facility, Corcoran II, and Bittaker at the Condemned Visitation block, San Quentin.

9.2 Dentures and a broken tooth that Norris sent to William. The postcard has a diagram of where the tooth broke, and Norris has written "This tooth broke on the State Oatmeal Cookie!" [Over the page.]

Ray T. Norris, C-30231
P.O. Box 5242, E-3/121
Corcoran, CA 93212

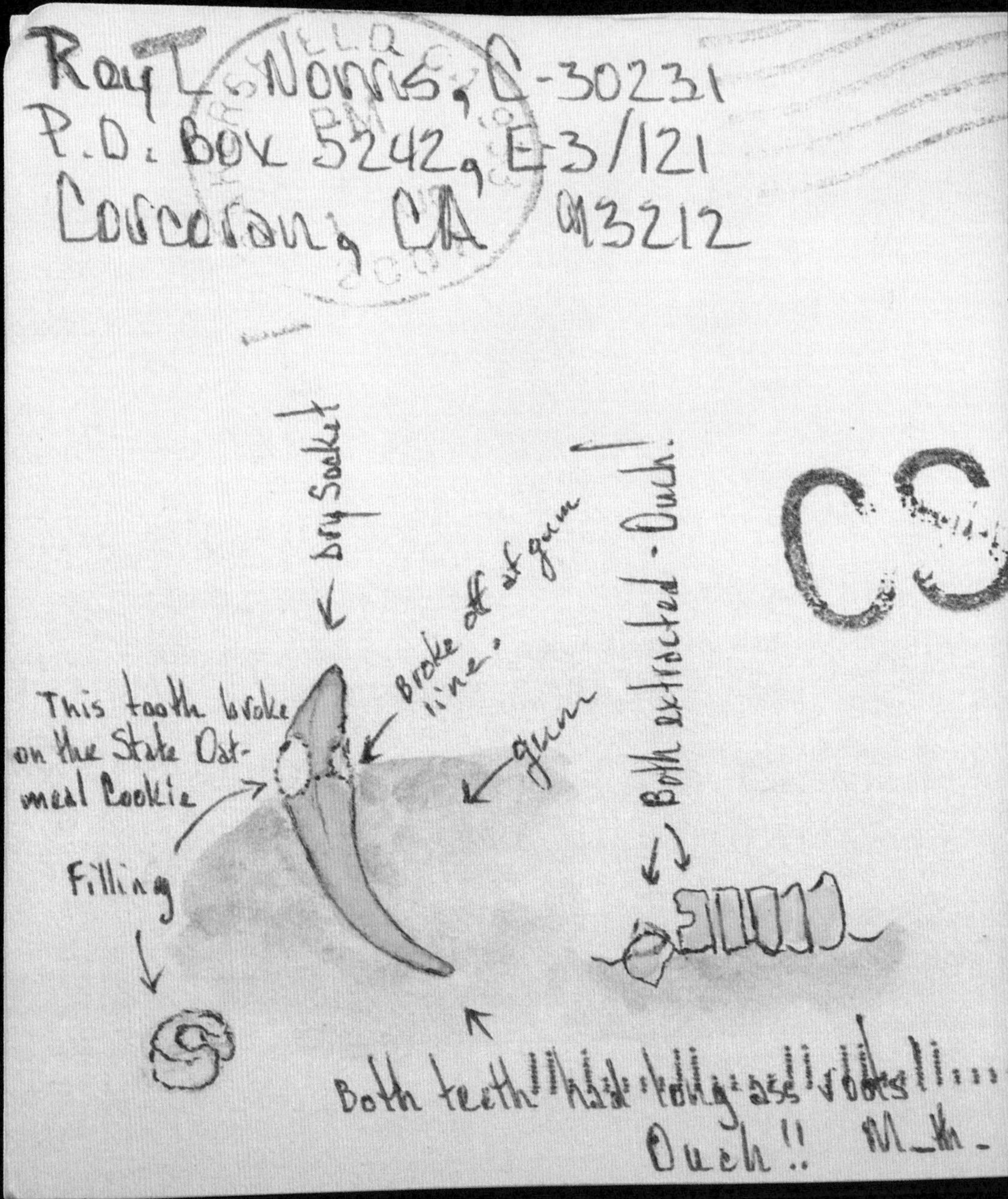

← Dry Socket

This tooth broke
on the State Oat-
meal Cookie →

Broke off at gum
line.

← gum

← Both extracted - Ouch!

Filling

Both teeth had long ass roots!!....
Ouch!! M_th_

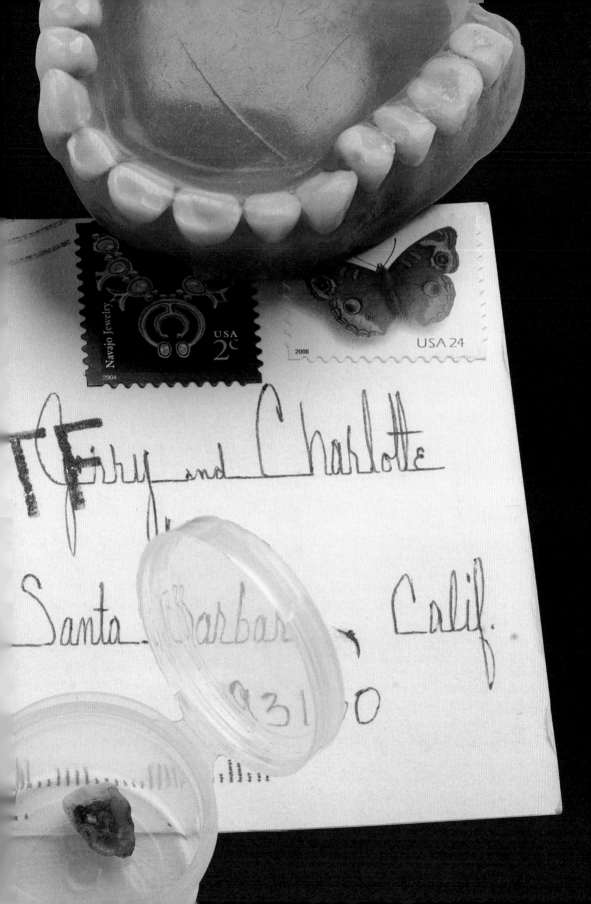

10. Wall of Sound

Legendary record producer Phil Spector, who changed music in the 1960s with his "Wall of Sound" production techniques, was serving a 19-year sentence for the 2003 murder of actress Lana Clarkson when he died of complications relating to COVID-19 in January 2021.

10.1 A greetings card and envelope from Phil Spector. "During my visits with Roy Norris and Gregory Miley, Phil Spector would always be seated directly next to us. I swear that guy sounds just like Mickey Mouse."

11. Cannibal's Chopsticks

When the convicted murderer and cannibal Issei Sagawa was set free on August 12, 1986, on a technicality, he was a "celebrity" in Japan, appearing in films, giving lecture tours, writing books and even food reviews. However, after the death of his parents in 2005, he claimed to dislike having to make a living on the reputation of his crime. In 2013, Sagawa was hospitalized with a cerebral infection, which permanently damaged his nervous system, rendering him an invalid.

11.1 Sagawa's signed palm print and (ominously) used chopsticks.

12. Killer Questions

Being convicted of raping and killing over 33 young men and burying them under your porch makes you very popular on the inmate pen-pal circuit. John Wayne Gacy had so many requests for correspondence that he composed a questionnaire for his potential "friends" to fill out and return.

12.1 A collection of Gacy questionnaires filled out and returned by pen pals. Questions include "why I wrote to John Wayne Gacy," "my biggest fear," and "what I don't like about other people." [Opposite and over the page.]

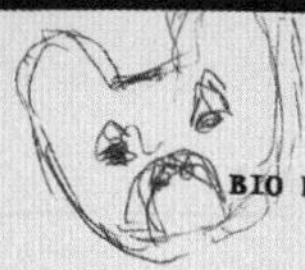

S

Full Name: _____

Age, Ht., Wt.: 42   5'5"   142

Date of Birth: FEb 19, 1951

Home: _____

Marital Status: YES - SOMETIMES

Family: YES -

Wheels: OLDS & HORSES (3)

Brothers: 0   Sisters: _____

Most Treasured Honor: _____

Perfect Woman or Man: NONE

Childhood Hero: RiN TiN TiN

Favorite TV Shows: _____

Favorite Movies: TOM JONES

Favorite Song: _____

Favorite Singers: _____

Favorite Musicians: _____

Hobbies: DOGS, KiDS - WON___

Favorite Meals: COQUE ST. JAC___

Why You Wrote JW Gacy: _____

Recommended Reading: _____

Last Book Read: WOMSMAN B___

Ideal Evening: _____

Every Jan. 1st, I Resolve: DiET AND NO SPENDING MONEY

Nobody Knows I'm: _____

My Biggest Regret: _____

If I Were President, I'd: CHANGE A LOT OF STUPID LAWS

My Advice to Children: STUDY iN School   READ, READ, READ

2/1/94

Bio Review

Date of Birth: 10/1/51 **A**

Ht., Wt.: 40, 5'4" 130   Home: FlA.

status: MARRied   Family: FlA

Dodge "STEALth   Brothers: 1   Sisters: 1

Treasured Honor: CRIMINAl JUSTICE AWARD

woman or man: STEVEN SEGAl

Childhood Hero: Dr. CASEY   Current Hero: NRA

TV shows: MURPhy BROWN

movies: The GodFATher

song: ComFoRTAbly Numb

singers: PAulA Abdul + miChAel BoltoN

Musicians: MiChAEl JACKSON -

Tennis -

Meals: - SAUSAGE + CAbbAGE

you wrote JW Gacy: I WAS inTEREsTED iN ARt AND SAW AN
article About you iN the PAPer

Recommended Reading: NoN FiCtioN

Book read: ON AFRiCA - ForGET the NAme

Evening: dinner out

Jan1st I resolve: To loSE weight

Everybody Knows I'm: yes they do - I'm AN open book!

Biggest regret: NoT EAtiNG Good

If I were President I'd: PRoviDE ShelTer FoR All the HomeleSS

advice to children: thiNk!

What I don't like about People: wheN they hurt Other people
OR ANimAls

Biggest Fear:
The wAter

Peeves: NAil bitiNG.

Superstitions: NoNe

friends like me because: I'm loyAl

INDEX

Picture credits

Dan Howell: the collections of Adam Crutchfield, Anthony Meoli, Casey Tillman, Geoff, Jerry G., Nathan, Robert Webb, Stephen J. Giannangelo, Dr. David R. Adamovich and Lynn J. Wheat, G. William Harder.
Kyle Jarrad: the collection of Brandy Williamson.
Rodney Montgomery: the collection of Devin Shomper.
Alexandre Halbardier: the collection of Nico Claux.

Author's acknowledgments

I would like to thank my wife Martine and son Anthony for dealing with me during the writing process (and when I'm not writing); all the people at Laurence King and Hachette for lending their amazing editing and visualization skills; and the collectors, who were gracious enough to allow me to photograph their extraordinary collections and share their personal insights into the world of true crime collecting.

About the author

Paul Gambino has been an avid collector of the macabre for over 20 years and owns an extensive collection of nineteenth-century memorial photographs. His two decades of collecting have gained him access to some of the world's most elite collectors of dark artifacts. His previous books include *Morbid Curiosities: Collections of the Uncommon and the Bizarre*, and *Skulls: Portraits of the Dead and the Stories They Tell*.

LAURENCE KING

First published in Great Britain in 2022
by Laurence King Publishing
an imprint of The Orion Publishing Group Ltd
Carmelite House, 50 Victoria Embankment
London EC4Y 0DZ

An Hachette UK Company

10 9 8 7 6 5 4 3 2 1

A CIP catalogue record for this book is
available from the British Library.

ISBN 978 0 85782 914 6

Design by Florian Michelet
Commissioning editor: Elen Jones
Senior editor: Gaynor Sermon
Origination by DL Imaging UK
Printed in China by C&C Offset Printing Co., Ltd.

Laurence King Publishing is committed
to ethical and sustainable production.
We are proud participants in the Book Chain Project®.
bookchainproject.com

www.laurenceking.com
www.orionbooks.co.uk